BUCKETS

How Business Legends Keep Their Hustlers

by Kevin D. Monaghan

DISCLAIMER PAGE

ISBN: 978-1-7353615-0-5
CRN: CRN202207-256691

DEDICATION

To G. Patrick and Deklin Patrick

Special Thank You:
Marie Tang, Editor

CONTACT INFORMATION

Kevin D. Monaghan
Intuitive Compensation Group LLC.
Kmonaghan@financialguide.com
(877) 705-3276

TABLE OF CONTENTS

CHAPTER ONE:
KEY EMPLOYEE

"If rewards do not work, what does? I recommend that employers pay workers well and fairly and then do everything possible to help them forget about money."
- Alfie Kohn[1]

Growing up I always wanted to be a comedian. Fresh out of college and full of enthusiasm, I moved to Los Angeles to pursue my dream. Youth and naivety got the best of me however and with my stand-up routine written and practiced only a handful of times, I decided it was time to get on stage.

To this day my first open mic experience is one of the most embarrassing moments of my life. If silence in a room could crescendo, it did that night. My three-minute routine, which felt more like one hundred and fifty minutes, was a complete and utter disaster.

My standup days were numbered before they even began but I'm no quitter and gave myself up to a new dream of being a comedy writer.

Eventually I worked my way up to being the writers' assistant for the NBC television show *'The Office'*. I was at the

---

[1] Alfie Kohn, AZ Quotes, 'Punished by Rewards',
https://www.azquotes.com/quote/1064720

doorstep of becoming a comedy writer. I was so close in fact, that I was physically in the room. I loved every minute of it and I felt truly fortunate to be part of the award-winning team.

Alas, as it was back then, and as you'll find out in this book, I'm not all that funny. In the end I never made it as a comedy writer. But I did take home a lesson from my stint on that show which still helps me today.

You see, I was in the presence of one of the ultimate key employees, Michael Scott, played by Steve Carell.

When we talk about compensation and the significance it has on keeping your most valuable players on board we need to recognize the impact of the key employee. Steve Carell signed on with 'The Office' right as his movie career began to take off. At the same time NBC began airing the show, Steve's first hit movie '40 Year Old Virgin,' was released. Steve was now regularly receiving more offers, for *more* money, just as any hot commodity employee would[2].

But Steve had signed a seven-year contract with NBC and would remain true to it. That seven-year tenure, which you will see in this book, has been forever imprinted on me for good reason.

I'm constantly reflecting on the impact Steve Carell had on so many lives in the period of time he spent on set as Michael Scott. He was NBC's key person and the writers' key person.

---

[2] Aramide Tinubu, What is Steve Carell's Net Worth? Here's What 'The Office' Icon Is Worth Today, ShowBiz Cheat Sheet, November 18, 2018, https://www.cheatsheet.com/entertainment/what-is-steve-carells-net-worth-heres-what-the-office-icon-is-worth-today.html/

Agents, producers, advertisers, actors, actresses, editors, set designers, make-up artists, executives, restaurants around the studio, and even my employment, was tied to him.

If Steve had decided to leave in Season Two, instead of serving all seven years of his contract, the "business" of television would not have played out for so many. NBC and all the actors who still receive residuals wouldn't be able to reap the windfall benefits they did. Moreover, the financial support hit shows like 'The Office' provide in finding the next big hit may not have been available had Steve broke his contract earlier than expected.

As with most things, the proof is in the pudding. After seven years on the set Steve Carell had fulfilled his contract with NBC. His resignation spurred a huge shift in the franchise. The very next episode after his departure saw viewership drop by almost 2 million. For the customer, the culture changed just as it had for me. I never quite regained my devotion to watching the show after he left. On the set, the culture had changed so much that the actors wound up approaching the writers to pitch an ending to the show.[3]

The departure of a key person can have a big impact on a company, its people and its profits. From start-ups to large corporations, losing a key player can change the game forever. Because once a key employee leaves, they may take with

[3] Thompson, Arienne. "Rain Wilson: 'The Office' Kinda Sucked After Steve Carell Left." USA Today. January 22, 3015.
https://www.usatoday.com/story/life/entertainthis/2015/01/22/rainn-wilson-the-office-kinda-sucked-after-steve-carell-left/77604532/

them the magic they brought to your organization. Just as it was with Steve Carell, once a key employee exits stage left, you may never get that magic back.

After leaving the comedy scene, I made my way to the metropolis of Shanghai, China. There I worked as a consultant and eventually led a team as a top producer for the firm. I was the key employee. The experiences I learned in that role and the undoing of the very lucrative company I had a hand in developing, was the basis for my current work seeking compensation retention solutions for business owners across America.

Ask anyone the first thing that comes to mind when they hear the word 'Compensation' and they will likely answer: **Money.** If you ask them what they consider as being 'Well Compensated,' they will likely answer: **A lot of money.**

It seems a simple enough formula for keeping an employee happy: *More Money = More Happy.* But what most business owners fail to recognize is that to an employee, there is no ceiling to 'a lot of money.' In addition to this, money is only part of the equation for what keeps key people retained.

With the rise of social media and industry conferences, it has never been easier for this era's workforce to seek better offers or pursue the lure of entrepreneurship. The result is business owners all over the world are rethinking what it means to keep their most valuable players on board. The age of digital nomads and 'selfies' have popularized the idea of 4-hour workweeks from the beach. And if your key employees are not content with what you have to offer, the "greener grass" is a mouse click away.

Research and countless studies have led us to discover exciting new ways to encourage retention. From in-house mindfulness workshops to beer taps in the office, to work-from-anywhere policies, businesses have been focusing hard on raising employee welfare and happiness. But while culture is a worthwhile motivator to invest in, fair compensation, in all its forms, will always be a major factor for whether your key person stays or goes.

This book is a collection of anecdotes that will get you thinking about compensation in a new way. My hope is that with the knowledge of how to compensate those valuable people in your company, you will be less likely to fall victim to the same line of thinking that drives key employees to competing firms or heading out the door.

Together we will explore why traditional compensation methods are plagued with unintended consequences and create conflicts of interest that can demotivate your key employees. We will outline the rules for the new era of compensation, which I refer to as *Intuitive Compensation*, and learn how it can make your company leaders feel appreciated while shielding your best asset from competing offers. The ability to tune into modern strategies and tax laws will keep you from defaulting to "old-school" solutions.

For those business owners who master *Intuitive Compensation*, you'll see how your retention plan may simultaneously position you for the better as an owner. Whether you're looking to keep profits rolling in, remove yourself from the day to day, expand, transfer ownership, or be ready at any moment to bait a higher multiple with a potential buyer, the ability to retain your best people will make all the difference.

Finally, this book will provide actionable tools to help you improve in your pay negotiations today. I'll share with you some of the lesser known retention strategies available to all businesses. While these concepts may be considered complex at first, we'll cut through the particulars so you can consider adding them to your toolbox as a business owner and a leader.

Asking for *more* is on the tip of every employee's tongue, especially those who know their value to the company. So as an entrepreneur, how will you strike the balance between what keeps your employees retained and what you can offer as an employer? How will you create a plan that combines your key employee's wants, needs, and what they think is fair? And, will it be enough to retain them tomorrow and the next day?

CHAPTER TWO:
TALE OF THE HUSTLER

"If you're a good leader, eventually,
their goal may be... to be you."
- Kevin D. Monaghan

The development of a key person in your organization means they were hired, trained and now execute the process you've laid out for them in a predictable way. They have an autonomy that allows you to trust things will run smoothly with little or no supervision. This in turn allows you to focus on other more important things in business and life.

Ironically, when everything is going well with this key person our brains are naturally wired to start worrying. As profits roll in that worry soon begins to turn into fear. A fear that they will leave.

While many seek a cure for key person turnover, it shouldn't come as a surprise that one doesn't exist, at least not in the way we wish it did. There is no magic formula you can use that will keep a key person. What works for one company won't work at another; what works for one employee, won't work for the next; and what works one year, may not work the following year.

When retention is the main goal, compensation discussions with key people can carry a lot of weight. The Six Pillars of Compensation you will learn about in this book, combined with the 10 Insights of *Intuitive Compensation,* will help you select the tools of your offering. To make your negotiation strategy even more impactful you'll also learn why your key people feel the need to ask for *more* in the first place.

Overall, we see the desire for *more* being expressed by key employees time and time again, even when they don't need it. And when you give them *more,* it only scratches the itch but doesn't heal it. This leads to a pattern of returning to ask for *more.* So how does one cure this?

Experts on the topics of motivating and rewarding people have written books sharing their findings about paying someone *more.* Daniel Pink's book, *"Drive: The Surprising Truth About What Motivates Us"* took the results of studies and found that compensation should be cognizant of intrinsic motivations, avoid "if-then" rewards, and focus on autonomy.[4] Steven Covey defines how to "think win-win" in your negotiations, easier said than done when it comes to compensation, in the *Seven Habits of Highly Effective People*[5] and in *Good to Great,* Jim Collin's proclaims that compensation should focus on retention and keeping the right people on the bus[6].

These are all valuable insights, but these books all turn to a cultural solution when it comes to retention. What about solu-

---

[4] Pink, Daniel. Drive: The Surprising Truth About What Motivates Us. New York: Riverhead Books, 2011

[5] Stephen R. Covey. The Seven Habits of Highly Effective People: Powerful Lessons in Personal Change. (New York: Free Press, 1989).

[6] Jim Collins. Good to Great: Why Some Companies Make the Leap...And Others Don't. (Harper Business, 2011).

tions when it comes to money? Rather than defer to a subject matter expert, I will share something Bono of the band U2 said during an interview on the Larry King Live show. Bono may have inadvertently summed up the viewpoint most business owners miss when it comes to compensation:

> 'In the United States you look at the guy that lives in the mansion on the hill and you think, you know, one day, if I work really hard I could live in that mansion. In Ireland people look up at the guy in the mansion on the hill and go, one day, I'm going to get that bastard.'[7]

The story describes two different points of view from the people below looking up at the successful mansion owner, and yes, most key people see the owner as "the guy in the mansion." Both points of view show envy for the person currently living in that mansion, but they are tied to different emotions. While one perspective illustrates resentment, the other describes a type of person who wants an opportunity to have what you have. In other words, to be you.

You're probably thinking, "They can dream all they want but I'm the one taking all the risk, using my resources and filtering *my* money back into the business. They can't be me." And you're right. The catch is though, you still want that key employee to be as good as you are and help grow your business. For that to happen you have to recognize that this

---

[7] Bono, Interview by Larry King, CNN Larry King Weekend, Cable News Network LP, LLC, December 1, 2002.

"dream," whether it be in the form of self-awareness or jealousy, can be a powerful motivating force.

After having this conversation many times with countless business owners and key employees, the simplest way to summarize the stance of the key person is this: They don't want to feel jealous of you, nor do they want to feel taken advantage of. What they want is to not think about pay. They want you to be a great leader in compensation, so they feel appreciated and part of something great.

Let's view this through the lens of a business owner to give you a better perspective of how this _feels_ for a key employee. This is the hypothetical story of the Hustler, the Producer, and the Legend.

The Hustler is a business owner that represents about 80% of all business owners. The Hustler exchanges time for money, just like a job does. In fact, that's precisely what they have, a job where they are the boss. The Hustler income ranges from losing money to earning up to roughly $300,000, mostly though, every penny is going right back into the business. They spend most of their time hunting, looking for a kill so they can eat. Once they've eaten, it doesn't take long for hunger to set back in and the scramble for the next meal begins. It's a cycle that continues in all aspects of business for the Hustler. Save, save, save, then spend. Feast, then famine. Feel relaxed for a few days, then right back into stress mode. The Hustler may have a few employees, one of which may be a key person, but most often the Hustler _is_ the key employee of their organization. Without the Hustler there is no business. The Hustler's biggest fear? Running out of money or time and never "making it."

The Producer represents about 17% of all business owners and is basically a Hustler who has achieved the dream and "made it". The typical Producer has $1 million to $100's of millions in revenue of which income is a controllable $300k to millions in profit. A Producer typically reduces their taxable income by purchasing equipment, trucks, property, investments, planes or dishing out bonuses at year end. The Producer, however, must still go to work most days and "produce," but it's not a stressful environment as it was back in the Hustler days. Producers typically have 5 to 100 full time employees helping them out, but usually a few key people are really making an impact to the top and bottom line. The biggest fear of the Producer? Losing a key person or two and having to go back to being and doing the activity of a Hustler.

The Legend on the other hand represents only about 3% of business owners. The Legend has effectively removed themselves from most or all of the day to day operations. Decisions for the Legend are made independent of their involvement, even big ones. Revenues can be anywhere from $2 million to $100's of millions. The Legend has a firm leadership team in place. The biggest fear of the Legend? Losing a chunk of their leadership team or a key person with solid connections to the business' largest clients. A loss here could send the Legend sliding down the ranks, costing them a lot of time, money, and opportunity. A Legend has the most to lose.

If an owner falls from the ranks of Producer or Legend, back to being a Hustler again, it can take a real toll emotionally and financially. Worse yet, there is no guarantee one will ever return to the highly prized status.

Now, imagine your first business taking off and you're a Hustler who is about to become a Producer. You've had a key employee who joined the organization early on in the Hustler phase. This key person winds up creating a Hustler's bond with you as you work side by side in the business. There is a shared sense of success when working together to build something great, even though they don't own the business. When the Hustler finally graduates to become a Producer, your key employee doesn't. They feel left behind as the Hustler's bond is broken. The key employee's biggest fear? An awareness that they are stuck in the Hustler phase, under your control, while they watch you reap the rewards of the higher levels.

Why do key employees want *more*? It's simple. They want a sense that they can have a bit of what you have. They want a shot at being the guy in the mansion; they want to feel that you are going to make them a Producer or a Legend.

The bad news is that a business is normally only capable of producing *one* Producer or Legend. The good news is they don't actually need to be a Producer or Legend for you to treat them like one. You can achieve this for your key person while at the same time protecting your hard-earned status.

If you could design a compensation package that made your key employee feel like a Producer or Legend, would you do it? A package that allowed them to feel pride as a provider for their family, would you do it? And what if in exchange for your generosity you were simultaneously incentivizing their retention which protected your own status and profits? Would you be able to get behind that type of compensation package?

Go one step further: what if your leadership brought this to your key employee, before they even asked, and you could avoid altogether them feeling jealous or taken advantage of? Establishing the right program, at the right time, can make your leadership stand out in your organization. It is the essence of *Intuitive Compensation*.

CHAPTER THREE:
WHAT IS INTUITIVE COMPENSATION?

"Employers handle the money –
it is the customers who pay the wages"
- Henry Ford[8]

One of the most successful business owners in American history didn't make his mark solely on invention. While Henry Ford is known for the Model T and its famous production line, he placed great value in human capital, making him a leader in what I call *Intuitive Compensation*. Ford was an inspiration to many by going against the grain and paying his workers more money, with less hours on the assembly line, without losing productivity[9].

It might be said that before things like 401k's and profit-sharing plans, life was simpler. You worked, you fed the family and you received a pension for retirement. But what Ford stumbled upon was that higher pay alone wasn't the greatest motivator. He recognized that by being in touch with employee's needs and knowing how to help them reach their personal

---

[8] Henry Ford, Due.com, July 1, 2015, https://due.com/blog/henry-ford-customers-pay-the-wages/
[9] Farnaz Hedayati, "3 Leadership Qualities of Henry Ford," Center for Work Life, May 7 2014, http://www.centerforworklife.com/leadership-qualities-henry-ford/.

and professional goals by increasing wages and offering reasonable hours he could motivate and retain them. This simple formula changed the shape of workplace practices and earned him a name for his exceptional leadership qualities.

In today's media driven society the needs of the employee have changed along with the means to save money. But what Ford intuitively understood about human nature is a major factor in running a successful business. You may have sowed the seeds, but your employees are tending the field. And if you want to keep them productive and motivated, so they continue harvesting the land, you're going to have to spend some time thinking outside of the (box) farm.

Like you, your employees seek quality of life. To do this, you will have to look at compensation with an abundance mentality. As a leader, you will need to invest in your key people which builds social capital within your organization. This in turn will compound results over time.

Safety + Trust + Time + Appreciation = Social Capital.

Notice money isn't in that formula? That's because it averages somewhere around fifth on the list of what's most important to key people.[10] Compensation that intends to retain top producers, should try and best factor in more elements of Social Capital rather than reward monetarily.

---

[10] "Verifying Motivators." Leading Answers. December 14, 2006. https://leadinganswers.typepad.com/leading_answers/2006/12/verifying_ motiv.html.

When we factor in the elements of interpersonal relation-ships, a shared sense of identity, shared norms and shared values, along with trust, cooperation, and reciprocity we are creating a foundation for *Intuitive Compensation*. The goal of this foundation is to help you prepare for the conversation with your key employees.

The chart below gives you an idea of what most business owners traditionally think of when creating compensation plans. Beside it is what business owners *should be* taking into consideration when it comes to *Intuitive Compensation*.

Traditional Compensation	Intuitive Compensation
Money	Appreciation
Rewards	Retention
IQ	EQ
Ownership	Wealth
Reactive	Proactive
Owner-led	3rd Party led
Profit sharing	Commitment
Long Term	5-10 Years
Retirement 59 ½	Shorter Term Goals
Unintentional Conflicts of Interest	Clarity
Owner Dictates	Treated as Equals

The structure of *Intuitive Compensation* also has ten thought provoking questions to challenge the traditional thought processes of how one should approach increasing overall pay. This list of ten does not represent ironclad rules that must be followed to a tee, because trying to force each one into your compensation strategy wouldn't work. To use them effectively you must treat them more like a guideline in preparation for your proposal to a key person.

Ten Intuitive Compensation Questions

1. Before I give them *more,* is this person retained?
2. Does my idea promote Producer or Legend type wealth for this person?
3. How does my compensation plan ensure they are learning & growing going forward?
4. Has my compensation plan connected with them emotionally (EQ), or is it just a good idea? (IQ)
5. Am I bringing this to them or am I responding to them?
   a. If I'm responding, how can I turn this around?
6. Who is leading this meeting: me or a 3rd party?
7. Does my plan commit today or is it promised based in an "if, then" scenario?
   a. "If, then's" are okay; best done after the person is retained.
8. Are my time frame expectations reasonable with this employee? (promote 5-10 years of tenure)
9. Am I incentivizing behaviors that may change their daily behaviors?
10. Under this plan is there a scenario where they can get nothing?

The main purpose here is to create a separation of feelings, seeking to avoid the elements altogether that makes a key person feel jealous and trapped as a Hustler within your firm while you thrive as a Producer or Legend. As a leader this navigation is crucial.

If you can treat your key employee like an equal, let them ebb and flow as your business changes without worrying about short term performance, then you will not only inspire results in your business, but you may allow a personal friendship to flourish as well. The *Intuitive Compensation* system is designed with this in mind.

CHAPTER FOUR:
THE RETENTION "*IDEAL ZONE*"

"Take away my factories, my plants; take away my railroads, my ships, my transportation, take away my money; strip me of all of these but leave me my key employees, and in two or three years, I will have them all again"
- Andrew Carnegie[11]

Some of you reading this book already have tenured leaders, especially if you've achieved Legend status, but some of you may be a Hustler or Producer and for the first time, fear losing someone that would set you back in time, energy and revenues.

While "anytime" is the correct answer to when retention strategies can be implemented, there is an ideal time of when, *when,* is "ripe."

---

[11] Benjamin Balbuena Aguenza and Ahmad Puad Mat Som, "Motivational Factors of Employee Retention and Engagement in Organization, Management Journal, Nov-Dec 2012, https://www.managementjournal.info/index.php/IJAME/article/viewFile/233/222

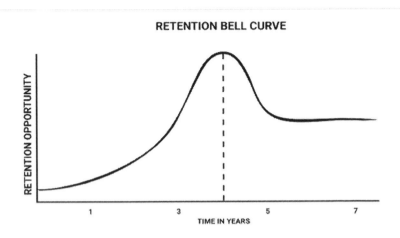

The chart above highlights the ideal time for a business owner to position for retention with a key employee. A dentist may peak between year 2-3, whereas a high-ticket sales advisor may take 5-7 years to reach full maturity and become a key player. While the peak may be different for each industry, or sometimes even based on the person, the upswing of the curve is typically the best time to retain them.

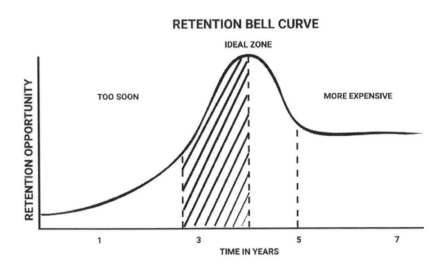

If you retain them too soon you risk the fact that they may have looked good on paper, but just didn't fit into the culture or processes of the firm. Wait too long and it can be much costlier to retain someone into the future.

As a general rule of thumb, we suggest key people should be <u>confirmed</u> as a key performer within your organization before you seek to retain them. Know their numbers and how they impact your bottom line. Make sure they are a key person not only in your eyes, but in everyone else's too.

The "ideal zone" represents their appreciation for your company, leadership and processes. At this stage in their tenure they are still grateful to you and have less reason to doubt their worth in the organization. This is the time implementing retention compensation is the easiest.

Once the *"ideal zone"* has passed, you are now entering a territory of being <u>reactive</u> in addressing your key people. It can still be done, don't get me wrong, but now, egos are bigger and retention could be more expensive to achieve. If you don't discuss compensation at this time a force inside your key person will start brewing, prompting the need to ask for *more*. This is what you want to avoid.

If your key employee is coming to you and asking for *more*, you must now realize that you are behind the curve with your leadership in this area. The most important awareness now is that most likely they have been stressing about *more*, for months, maybe even years. The longer defining *more* goes unaddressed, or remains open-ended, the more damage may be done.

Additionally, when past the *"ideal zone,"* you'll see the need for your leadership skills to rise to new heights. Because your key person will be acting out of emotion and may not have the necessary skills to communicate their wants in an efficient way, they may come off as demanding or ungrateful. Being cognizant of the "*ideal zone*," will help you avoid you having to take it on the chin altogether when these situations arise.

Here, you will need to fight instincts that will usually send both parties into a scarcity mentality, as these conversations test the bond you thought you had with this person. For example, the relationship between a business owner and her key employee who helped build the company from the ground up, now becomes strictly a business decision with both sides positioned on the defensive. It can be fixed, but as an owner, you will have to take the high road and find a solution, especially if this employee is vital to your organization.

The chart below represents how a top producer's thought process changes as they move past the "*ideal zone*" and move from appreciation to "what's in it for me?"

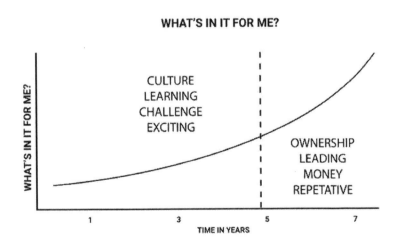

WHAT'S IN IT FOR ME?

What the key employee experiences when they pass the "ideal zone" is fear of remaining a Hustler for the long haul. They have no control over the business to change their Hustler status and they begin seeing their work as not challenging and mundane. So now they want *more* to compensate for these stuck-in-a-rut feelings. Money will not fix this void, but it will be the default requirement when that awkward conversation comes to your office.

While it is not always a negative to pass the "ideal zone" it may set the stage for a more expensive solution. If you wait too long you could now be competing against outside forces. Your key person may have received a job offer by your competitor or begun to draft out plans for starting their own business. Therefore, your offer may have to be much *more* in order to keep them because it might be competing against an alternative already planted in their mind.

What's the worst part? If they do ask for *more*, and you give it to them in an attempt to retain them, you've set a precedent for them and the other employees. It shouldn't be a surprise, then, when they come back (sooner than expected in most cases) and ask for *more* again.

This is why getting the *when* right is so important.

CHAPTER FIVE:
GETTING IT RIGHT

"Experience is the best,
but most expensive form of compensation."
- Kevin D. Monaghan

My Journey

Premier International Group is getting ready for its annual leadership meeting. In the boardroom of our new penthouse office suite in Shanghai's bustling business district, everyone is eager to commence the long overdue meeting.

Countless distractions, an office move, and a constant "hustle" to grow revenues led to continual delays of a compensation meeting between the owners and their Rockstar producers (myself included). But it was on everyone's minds.

After 5 years of team hustle the key employees wanted to know who was responsible for the incoming revenue and what their reward for bringing it in would be.

While we wait I gaze out of the window overlooking the rooftop of the Shangri-La hotel. I'm distracted to say the least. Just two days earlier a competing firm offered me a position running their firm in Thailand. It was a chance encounter at an event, but within 3 minutes of meeting me, the CEO of the firm had made me an offer.

Being handed a lucrative job offer wasn't some fluke though. My co-manager Pierre and I were gaining a reputation in Shanghai as leaders in the field of financial consulting. Being that the expat community was still relatively small, the deals we were closing were not going unnoticed.

I cut my teeth with Premier International Group and had no plans to jump ship, but nonetheless it was tempting to have a big offer for which I didn't even have to hold an interview. The offer gave me an entrepreneurial rush that felt good, and, if I'm to be frank, it was a major ego boost. Having put so much into this company, I felt obligated to see what Chris and Mike, the owners, had in store for my future with them.

"Kevin, what do you think?" The owners walked in and I didn't even notice.

"Sorry, about what?"

"All expense paid trips for the gang to Thailand next month?"

Sure they were joking, but if they only knew...

Every business dives into a similar meeting with its leadership team to determine goals and incentives. Its core purpose is to address an underlying question that all partners, owners, investors and key employees everywhere wish to know. "What's in it for me?" Our international consulting firm was no exception.

It was apparent to everyone in the company that Pierre and I were the major contributors in getting the company to where it was. The fact that we were targets for being poached was never discussed in the open, but Chris and Mike knew the industry had no qualms about employee raiding and they wanted to make sure we were retained.

The owners had a plan for facing our toughest questions, one they thought would work, but we had some frustrations as well. Mainly, while our work was providing the owners with Legend status, we felt stuck as Hustlers. Eighteen months prior, a meeting like this resulted in myself and Pierre receiving 10% equity. And now, Pierre was asking for *more*. As one of the company's leaders, he felt he deserved this extra slice of the pie, but if we're talking numbers, Pierre was actually being outperformed by the younger protégé he himself trained. Ironically, Kyle, the rising star and current top producer in the firm was sitting right beside us wondering what he should be asking for.

For me, the 10% we currently owned provided no distributions and no control. I couldn't sell it, nor did I have access to check the books or make decisions on any portion of it. To me, my 10% equity stake was about as valuable and as useful as owning a small percentage of my neighbor's couch. I couldn't reupholster my 10%, or even have free access to my neighbor's home to use it. Another 5% would be just as worthless as the first 10% to me. Still, I was drawn into the meeting, intrigued by how intent Pierre was on getting his extra equity.

"Should we fire Pierre and give his equity to Kyle?" a poorly timed joke by the owners, but as they say, there's truth in jest. It might have actually been the correct move. Fortunately for Pierre, equity doesn't exchange so freely based on the value of current contribution. Hence, why constantly reevaluating equity splits, as suggested in the book *Slicing Pie* by Mike Moyer, causes too many subjective arguments to be effective for most.

"Not for nothing but I have been working my ass off and I think I deserve equity too," Kyle chimed in.

The attention turned to the eloquent 27 year old who was now using his production numbers as evidence as to why he should receive more equity than Pierre, who trained him.

The conversation was becoming more and more heated. Pierre had no choice now but to cling to his self-importance for recruiting the protégé in the first place.

While the conversation continued to focus on equity, I was beginning to see that the entire negotiation was moot point. The value of the shares we held had no value anyways, as no one wanted to buy these shares. The only people who wanted the shares were the up-and-coming key employees, who wanted shares the same way we got it: For free.

As the level of frustration and "importance positioning" were increasing, the scarcity and defensive mindsets began to set in on both sides.

Chris and Mike do not necessarily want to give away more equity, but they realize the bind they're in. It also brings back feelings of their own experiences as top producers and the discontent that came from not getting what they felt they de-served. And they remembered what they did when they were in those shoes, they left.

The owners proposed that they could only do *more,* in the form of a profit-sharing plan, if we increased production. This meant *more* delay for the key players. Leaving a meeting where defining *more* is postponed into the future is simply not a good idea. This delay tactic often leads to the initial thoughts of a key person wanting to leave.

Compensation should be treated as a skill set needed to create and maintain personal and business relationships. And despite having the best intentions on 'getting it right' (no one wants to jeopardize profit), business owners often get it wrong. By missing the mark with key people, you risk your compensation strategy leading to trust issues and resentment with people who were once proud to be working for you. This could lead to a drop-in performance and instigate a search for greener pastures.

The owners of Premier International Group broke many of the principles of *Intuitive Compensation* but one stands out in particular. They were *reactive* instead of *proactive*. The equity they gave early on as an incentive didn't work and rather than acknowledging this, they brought to the table a profit-sharing solution if performance improved, which came off as in insult. While it may have been a good idea (intelligent quotient (IQ)) in theory, was not received that way by the key people (an emotional quotient *(EQ)* misread).

When an owner becomes too "busy" or goes too long without being tuned in to where compensation stands on the minds of their key people, adverse reactions can build up quickly. Being *proactive* with your compensation can make you a differentiator in your market, your people, and allow you to stand out.

Take a look at another company's experience in Asia. In Singapore, Uber, who was first to market and had a dominant market share, was sent packing by the competition who was proactive with their compensation.

Grab, a competitor, had raised a lot of money to compete with Uber in Singapore. Despite touting a superior offering and technology, it was not well received as drivers loathed switching when Uber was so well known. Being *proactive* and tuned into the *E.Q.* of what could impact drivers' lives, Grab found an edge that turned the tables and allowed them to start "grabbing" market share.

Uber, who thought in traditional methods of compensation, paid their drivers every Monday[12]. Weekly pay is very common, with a long tradition of doing so. Grab realized drivers were looking to make fast money and decided to run payroll 2x a day[13]. When drivers learned money would be in their bank accounts the minute they finished their shifts, it was a non-brainer to switch companies.

In less than two years Uber announced it was exiting the Singapore market. Ultimately, they wound up joining forces with Grab by taking a minority stake. When it comes to compensation being a forward thinker may be the thing that separates you from your competitors.

The owners of Premier International Group got tangled in the vines of traditional compensation. Ultimately, the owners never got it right in Shanghai and the conflicts wound up destroying a lot of potential wealth for all of us. We were all so close to securing Producer and Legend status for the long term but the owners, managers, rising stars and myself, all fell down the ranks back to being Hustlers.

Those who find comfort in traditional compensation thinking, simply see things too late.

---

[12] "When Does Uber Pay Its Drivers," First Lane, January 30, 2018, https://www.firstlane.com.sg/uber-pay-drivers/

[13] Kim Jio "When Does Grab Pay Its Drivers," First Lane, February 7, 2018, https://www.firstlane.com.sg/grab-pay-drivers/

CHAPTER SIX:
ASK. SURVEY. REALITY.

"Buyers are liars"... and unfortunately, so are your key people."
- Kevin D. Monaghan

Perhaps the most powerful awareness when it comes to compensation negotiation is the ability to understand the wisdom behind what I refer to as "Ask me. Survey me. Reality." In other words, asking employees what they want will give you one answer and reviewing survey data on what employees say they want, will yield a different answer. And then the reality of what plays out, is something different altogether.

When it comes to negotiating and making an offer in compensation, if you're not careful, the first two could give you a false positive for the reality of what will make them stay.

"New Coke," Burger King French Fries, and the making of the movie Poseidon, all experienced positive results when asking and surveying customers. But as we all know, the reality was "poor taste," lack of a timeless staple and a film "underwater."[14] [15] [16]

---

[14] The Real Story of New Coke. 2012. https://www.coca-colacompany.com/history/the-real-story-of-new-coke

[15] Nassauer, Sarah. "Burger King Tries New French Fries." The Wall Street Journal. September 23, 2013. https://www.wsj.com/articles/burger-king-tries-new-french-fries-1379989427

To see how this theory plays out, we can turn to almost any industry. Take the Energy Sector for example. Power plants have long been faced with the challenge of reducing greenhouse gasses. As regulation on emissions continues to increase, energy companies have been forced to seek ways to encourage lower consumer usage[17]. Power plants are forced to address the increasing demands of society while struggling to extend the use of existing facilities.

Energy companies set out to reduce consumer usage and began by sending out _surveys_ asking customers what they cared about that would inspire them to use less energy. When surveyed, customers responded overwhelmingly that they cared about the environment.

The energy company, armed with this information, sent out the next monthly billing statements with a surprise. They plastered the bills with statistics on how much impact you would make on the environment if you used less energy. In bold letters and big fonts, the energy bill displayed the stats on how turning the air conditioners up two degrees while at work, could save many trees. Saving trees meant acres of rain-forests would be spared and that in turn generated the amount of CO_2 your reduced carbon footprint saved.

---

[16] _Poseidon._ Bomb Report. 2019. https://bombreport.com/yearly-breakdowns/2006-3/poseidon/

[17] Mark Joseph Stern, "A Little Guilt, A Lot of Energy Savings," Slate, March 01, 2013, https://slate.com/technology/2013/03/opower-using-smiley-faces-and-peer-pressure-to-save-the-planet.html

---

The result of the campaign? Flat. No real impact on energy consumption was recorded. Turns out saving the environment is something everyone *says* they care a lot about. The reality was, what the survey respondents directly told them would work, didn't.

Next, the energy companies hit the phones and *asked* their customers what it would take to get them to reduce their energy bills. The response... money. Consumers said they wanted lower energy bills. So in response to this, when the monthly billing statements went out, they were filled with money savings statistics quantifying how much turning the lights off or having the air conditioner up a few degrees at peak times, could save. The result? The needle didn't budge. Asking customers directly what it would take to get them to reduce energy usage, didn't work.

Frustrated, the energy companies turned to experts in human behavior. They came up with a few ideas, one of them being a chart that would illustrate how much energy a customer was using as compared to their neighbors. The result? Success.

Residents who became aware of how much they were using began to feel guilty. And for many, whether or it was guilt or the need to compete with their neighbors, it was the motivation they needed to make changes in their energy consumption.

The takeaway? The *reality* of what drove results was something that consumers couldn't communicate.

No truer does this concept apply than to compensation. When *surveyed* employees will say they want to be appreciated, challenged, and a part of something greater than themselves.

When _asked_ they will say they want _more_ money, _more_ equity or _more_ profit sharing.[18] Sure their input is important, but will the _reality_ of what they tell you really be effective when it comes to keeping your key employees?

Honing in on your employees _reality_ and their circumstances, and zeroing in on what it will actually take to keep them over time will be one of the most difficult things you will do as a leader. And when you give them what they want and it doesn't work out, nothing will be more frustrating.

On the other side of the table your key employee goes into a compensation negotiation wondering "Will my raise be bigger than last year?" "Will I get partner or equity?" "how much did Jane get?" "I deserve more." These thoughts can occupy a lot of head space for your key people. The hard part is navigating between what you think is _fair_, and their expectations of what is _fair_.

Give them too much and it can haunt you going forward by setting a high precedent and making it difficult to navigate lower amounts in the future. Offer too little and risk disgruntled employees who become unproductive and seek other opportunities. If they had a great year, they may even get bold in their suggestions with you, while conveniently discounting the years of training and losses you took in developing them.

No matter what the circumstances are, your key employee is looking for you to be a leader who gets compensation right.

---

[18] "Verifying Motivators." Leading Answers. December 14, 2006.
https://leadinganswers.typepad.com/leading_answers/2006/12/verifying_
motiv.html

They'll respect you for it and that appreciation will trickle down through the ranks of the company.

Owners tend to adapt the guidelines of *Traditional Compensation* when it finally comes time to meet with our key person about money. In my years of consulting, I've bared witness to some of the most creative, elaborate excel spreadsheets, all designed to align performance goals with potential rewards. Naturally, we seek solutions that expose us to the least amount of increased overhead and keeps the harmony with our all-stars.

Some owners spend hours and hours of preparation time on the perfect pitch to their key people on why their proposal is a "fair" solution. Plans are laid out for bonus structures, equity plans, buy-ins, profit sharing plans, all with the intent of outlining how employees can make more money for their efforts.

When it finally comes time to present your idea to a key employee, they may surprise you with an ace up their sleeve. Contrary to what you think is coming their weapon of choice is often not derived from citing performance statistics or an ability to negotiate back and forth. What I am warning about is probably not what you are expecting at all.

Their bargaining tactic is going to be to say "yes."

You are reading this correctly. Your key employee giving you a "yes" and agreeing to your proposal is the best negotiation tool they have. Seems like you would win if your proposal receives a "yes," doesn't it? Not so fast.

For "*key employee math,*" it looks like this:

Proposal + "Yes" = Take Now, Adjust Later

This is why the _reality_ of what will work, versus what they tell you will work, may not actually work. This is why you hear of so many key people with equity, that _still_ wind up leaving. A key employee will likely say "yes" to any plan that promises _more._ It may be after a few painful back and forth conversations, but if they say "yes" and are later unhappy with how it's playing out, then they will simply cite the negatives and come back asking for _more._

To address this we must turn not to money, but instead emotion. In countless books and studies, we learn that the best motivation comes from deep within us.[19] In the film Inception, a team of influencers would sneak into the minds of corporate executives to plant ideas deep within their subconscious. Once that thought is inside their mind, and if it catches within the subconscious, a deep drive influences the executive to move towards it, even against all odds. Once the subconscious mind is on board, our conscious brain knows what to do.

What _Intuitive Compensation_ looks to achieve is to intentionally turn the tables during the compensation negotiation. When the solution _feels_ like it was created by the key employee, with a process that connects their goals to their _reality_, then it is possible to align their emotions with their retention. An idea that is our own, creates our strongest motivation. With _Intuitive Compensation_, your retention strategy comes off as their idea.

---

[19] Alison Eldrige, _Inception_, Encyclopedia Britannica, July 23, 2012, https://www.britannica.com/topic/Inception

CHAPTER SEVEN:
THE 6 PILLARS OF COMPENSATION

1. Pay (Salary, Bonus, Commission)
2. Benefits
3. Equity
4. Profit/Revenue Share
5. Lawyering
6. Retention Compensation

1ST PILLAR: PAY

*"Whether fundamentally sound or not, someone is
always willing to throw more money at your employee,
to fix their problem."*
- Kevin D. Monaghan

Every year spawning salmon return to the same stream from which they were born. Their internal compass guides them to the spot where they will deposit their eggs and leave their mark for the season.

Something similar happens to your employees year in and year out. It seems that some annual calling leads them to your office every time they are due for a raise. Unfortunately for you, the business owner, this journey to the place they were given life (at least within your organization) doesn't take into consideration expenses, performance, revenues, profits or other visions you may have for your growing business. For the employee who's been around a few years, he's simply following his instincts. Get. My. Raise.

Society seems to have an unwritten rule that paying somebody the same or less than the year before is not allowed. To do so would mean their place of employment is blatantly trying to get them to leave. On top of that there is also an expectation that it will be a fair raise in accordance with *their* viewpoint of their value to your firm and how much they believe you've profited as a business throughout the course of the year.

Nevertheless, having this conversation with employees and committing to *more* each year is part of doing business.

When it comes to the first pillar of compensation, Pay, I will focus on three main ingredients: salary, bonuses and commissions.

Salary

Salary is the first ingredient in the Pillar of Pay and is typically the opening negotiation when hiring an employee. Tenure begins with a comfortable acceptance of what has been agreed upon as a fair, maybe even generous, salary. With that, everyone is bright eyed and ready to perform.

As your business grows and your employees become more vital to your day to day, salary alone somehow becomes hardly enough to stand on its own. In fact, it can become a benchmark for what they will ask for next in the form of a raise, or worse, their bottom-line for a competitor's offer.

This is what makes supporting retention with the First Pillar so difficult. On some level, salary for many of your employees will be market-based and you won't have much trouble retaining them as long as you keep to basic math. The way you compensate your key personnel however, is a whole other ball game.

With key personnel the stakes are higher. If they've proven themselves you're happy to bump up their pay in an effort to keep them happy. If they haven't been up to par in production or initiative for the year, a meager increase may offend them and have a negative impact on their performance.

Another seemingly common "buffer" many bosses tend to use is a marginal spread between what an employee is being paid against what the company could afford to pay them. I know this gap exists because in my meetings with owners where a key employee has left for a competitor offer, they will often admit, "I would have paid him more if he had just asked me!"

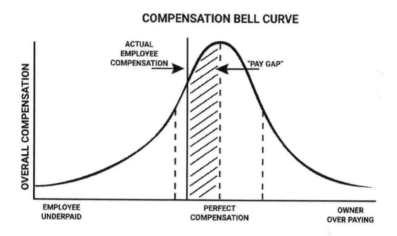

What this means is that many business owners keep a tab. For example, you may be paying your key person $68,000, but have it in mind that you could potentially be paying them $80,000. That spread allows you to be lulled into thinking you're getting a good deal because you feel you have room to offer more when that annual exodus into your office comes around. This again is a trap of traditional compensation thinking.

While it feels good to give a raise, even if it's a correction in your employees pay for the added work they picked up along the year, it may set the tone for the *employee math* that you may not be aware of at all.

Take the owner, who during a good year raised his rising key person's salary from $60,000 to $68,000. That's a 13.3.%

increase. While we may see this as a good raise, *employee math* equates this percentage as some sort of benchmark for the following year, and anything less than a 13.3% raise will be viewed as a negative. See what you get for being nice!

This cycle creates a few issues. First, you're setting precedent for big raises that will compound quickly on you. It will only take a few years until you're paying above industry averages and "surprise, surprise" the expectation for *more* still remains.

Secondly, paying people generously and increasing their salary trains them to jump at *more*. If a competitor comes along and offers more, they may see this as a reason to leave. Under other circumstances, you may need to start decreasing the big raises they've grown accustomed to, which might also provoke your key people to consider taking a higher offer elsewhere.

The more successful your company growth is, the more they expect the compounding salary raises to continue. The faster you grow, the more difficult it becomes to justify not paying them more.

As an owner, your main task is staying busy and keeping your eye on the prize. You want to reward everyone for their hard work, but often times bosses are so wrapped up in what they're doing that by the time they take a breath, they've painted themselves into a corner. Pay more and set a precedent for the future but keep the machine running? Or don't, and risk losing the people who churn the wheels.

Life would be so much easier if we could simply use a chart to decide what fair salary was and then give pay raises according to the CPI inflation index. Everyone would have clarity and be happy with predictable payroll expectations. Unfortunately, in a free market economy where all workers have their own skills and circumstances, such a solution doesn't exist. Therefore, in an effort to tackle salary increases we naturally invented the bonus system.

Bonuses

"We are going to be introducing a bonus at the end of this quarter," you say with a smile. Energy surges through the room. "If the company does well and we can hit our targets, we'll pay out a bonus based on how we do as a company."

What you're really saying is, "I'm tired of pay raises and I'm going to use bonuses as a better way to keep my overhead in check." But as you look around the room, everyone seems content and you officially have a new incentive in place.

What you forgot though is that "yes" is the path of least resistance for them.

The smiles are usually short lived. You presented to your team a way to compensate them based on the performance of the company as a whole, but what about individual performance? Does tenure, management, personal performance, department, or even external factors affect how much of a bonus everyone gets? There are a few problems we face when using a bonus structure when it comes to retention.

For one, the "bonus" in today's workplace society has become somewhat expected. Pay a bonus one year, and next year it becomes the standard. When asked, "what if you don't get a bonus this year?" a typical answer is, "we get it every year, they would never not pay it."

An owner selling farming equipment in Virginia told us that one year they paid a flat $1,000 bonus to all of their employees. They had done fairly well in sales that year and everyone was satisfied with the fair and reasonable bonus. The next year, the company did okay as a whole, but sales were down and money was being put into upgrading their product. This in turn generated a $500 bonus to each team member.

How do you suppose the staff reacted? Not only were employees starting to update their resumes because they thought the company was going under, but morale around the water-cooler was filled with complaints, worry and a general sense of negativity. Remember, you see one side and *employee math* sees another.

The problem with bonuses from the worker's perspective is that they create an expectation in their mind of what it should be. Remember in *National Lampoon's Christmas Vacation* when Clark Griswold put a down payment on a pool with the bonus he was expecting to receive and instead received a membership to the Jelly of the Month club?[20] If you don't meet or exceed the expectation employees have for a bonus, it can be a huge let down.

With no say over the company's books, employees tend to default to the dark side of *employee math*. First, they will expect a bonus that either matches or tops the one from the year before, every year. Second, they end up basing their expectations around things like your perceived lifestyle. Ever feel

---

[20] *National Lampoon's Christmas Vacation*, directed by Jeremiah S. Chechik (1989; Glendale, CA: Warner Bros, 1997), DVD.

judged when you buy a new car or truck with the company's funds, or maybe take a vacation or two during the year? "The company must be doing well, so I'm probably going to get a pretty decent bonus this year" becomes the go-to prediction. Unfortunately, when your books and your employees' expectations don't match up, you could risk employees' jumping ship or dragging your company culture through the mud.

Commission

Commission often creates an "eat what you kill" philosophy. With no caps on what you can earn, and in some cases no salary at all, commission-based work definitively challenges an employee to produce results.

As an owner, commission allows a clear negotiation when it comes to pay in that employees need to produce more to make *more*. It may be a problem for revenues if your top sales guys end up sleeping on the job, but at least you didn't overpay them.

With commission-based earning, your key person is in essence "free" to control much of what they do and how much they choose to earn. They are a pseudo business owner within your firm. A commissionable employee in return gets to avoid a lot of the headaches that come along with running a business, and just focus on one activity. In addition, commissions, partially or fully, can leave a person to self-manage themselves determining their own set of variables around their schedule, strengths, and income.

There is a downside to paying someone commission though, which unsurprisingly, comes in the form of ego. Once a person on commission becomes a performer and is bringing in the business, they quickly forget the value provided by the brand. All the things that got them to where they are, the company, territory, contacts, and the training they received, has been forgotten. It becomes easy for a high performing person to start throwing their weight around and complain about how they think things should be, especially if they are 100% compensated by commission.

Egos can get big fast and when ego's grow, the competition knows. Your top producers will be bombarded with incentives, higher rates and reminders of how green the grass is at your competitor's doorstep. Even in industries where commissions have been time tested and honed-in by free market checks and balances, there are still top performers who would bicker that they should get a larger slice of the pie.

It's a catch-22. Your company spends money training people to do great which leads some key employees to bring in solid numbers. At the same time, they become aware of their value to the firm which gives them power to demand *more*. Now, your investment in them can make you feel held hostage to their demands.

2ND PILLAR: BENEFITS

"…The weakest pillar. You either have them, or you don't…
If you don't, they'll argue the cost for more pay."
- Kevin D. Monaghan

Benefits represent the weakest pillar of compensation for a business owner and key employees. Group life, group health, short term disability, long term disability, retirement plans, etc. are the standard options.[21]

There is a cost to providing these benefits and as an owner you'll need to decide if you want to pay to provide that benefit or not. Most likely, you wind up paying for it anyway because if you don't provide the benefit for them, then the employee will have to take care of it on their own dime which may lead to them citing rising health care costs as another reason why they need a raise.

Do benefits work to keep employees? Perhaps, but benefits can have more of an impact on non-key-level employees than the top earners at your company. A person who is use to making hundreds of thousands a year, isn't stressed over handling a term life insurance payment, or missing out on a 3% retirement match.

---

[21] Griffin, Jeff. "10 Most Commonly Offered Employee Benefits." JP Griffin Group, February 17, 2017. https://www.griffinbenefits.com/blog/10-commonly-offered-employee-benefits

Any item in the benefits package could be bought for a price elsewhere. If you don't have group life insurance, it isn't too difficult to go online and get a quote for $250,000. My own sister was going from a big bank to a smaller start-up company. The smaller company didn't offer disability insurance, but all other benefits were similar. She priced out what a disability policy would cost, went back to the offering company and asked them if they could increase the offer so she could keep this important benefit in place for her family. They agreed; deal done.

The downfall of the benefits pillar is in the simplicity of the alternative offer:

Competitor Offer =
Salary Expectation + Cost of Missing Benefits + Incentive

3RD PILLAR: EQUITY

"Little minority shareholder – Little Fool.
Big minority shareholder – Big Fool."
- Albert Frere[22]

In 1973, childhood friends started a 50/50 partnership paving roads in rural Illinois. Young and ready for anything, the two friends got off to a good start, but weren't making much. Three years into the business, one of the partners tragically passed away. At only 27 years old, with a brand new family, the deceased partner's spouse inherited 50% of the company shares.

To this day, over four decades later, the spouse has never worked a day in the business. For over thirty years the surviving owner put his heart and soul into the company to honor his dear friend. In that time he was able to not only grow the business, but continued to pay out enough dividends to flow through to her 50% share. Those dividends supported his good friends' family their entire life.

With no agreements or terms written up at the time of his partner's passing he could have legally kept 100% of the profits. He had every right to give up the business, try to buy his

---

[22] "Albert Frere: Background and Bio," Value Walk Premium, 2018, https://valuewalkpremium.com/albert-frere-resource-page/

friend out, or, not pay any dividends at all. When I asked him about it, his only response was, "I gave him my word."

Imagine yourself in the same position. You may find it easy to say you would do the same, but in reality if you knew that in thirty years from now your business would grow to be a multi-million dollar conglomerate, would you, in <u>year three</u>, give 50% to a non-working entity?

Equity is the third pillar in our story. It is often seen as the "go-to" for many business owners when formulating retention plans for many reasons, but most commonly because it is easy to understand and execute. Because so many companies use equity to retain and incentivize key employees, it almost perpetuates itself as normal to do so. This is what lulls business owners into a false sense of security in giving equity away: *if others are doing it, it should work for me too.*

Make no mistake, if you give away equity in your company to a key employee, then you now have a business partner. However, a key employee is usually not a good business partner. If you give them 10%, don't expect them to help you when you invest $100,000 to buy that new million-dollar machine. Want to take on more debt? Minority shareholders may not want, or have the means to take any debt. And by the way, the banks may no longer count that 10% minority ownership when considering how much of a loan you'll qualify for. When you make a key person an equity partner, they want all the positives and none of the negatives. They expect their equity to be a free ride.

There are downsides for key employees too. Their equity usually has no market to sell other than to the owner. The only natural market is the next generation of leaders in the firm and they won't want to buy in, they want it the way their colleague got it, for free. So you can imagine how much "market" value those shares would hold, not much.

Not to imply all equity splits will go south, but there is certainly no shortage of stories of frustration and regret when it comes to partnerships and equity splits.

When I moved back to America, I was sure business partners would be more cordial and have a sense of camaraderie in working together for shared success than forced partnerships in China. I was wrong.

As the saying goes, "there's no interest like self-interest." When things take a turn for the worse in equity partnerships, the value of time invested, opportunity, and hard work can quickly crumble. What started out with good intentions, can quickly turn to mistrust and stalled opportunity. Under these circumstances stakeholders quickly turn to a scarcity mindset.

In other words, you might give away shares to a key player in your company today, only to realize in three years that they no longer play a vital role in your organization. This is the downside risk to equity. It would be like placing a huge bet on a champion thoroughbred for a race that's going to happen a few years from now. You just can't predict what will happen. Equity agreements can then lead to regret that may have a lasting impact on you and your business.

By issuing equity you're limiting your ability to control or shift value in the future. Like in the film *The Social Network,* the story of Facebook's start-up, your business could explode in value and leave you over paying an executive who barely put in anything close to the value extracted[23].

Equity ratios simply don't auto-adjust to reflect the ongoing performance or reality of the stakeholder's contribution. For that reason, equity splits may leave business owners vulnerable economically and emotionally.

---

[23] *The Social Network*, directed by David Fincher (2010; Andover, MA: Columbia Pictures, 2010), DVD.

4ᵀᴴ PILLAR: PROFIT-SHARING PLANS

"Profit sharing plans...
As many unintended consequences as politics."
- Kevin D. Monaghan

On the surface profit sharing plans should be the best form of compensation, and widely implemented with key employees. Profit-sharing allows an owner to put more pay on the table, without increasing the overhead payroll expense. These types of plans can also be an entrepreneurial form of compensation.

Profit-sharing should be an ideal opportunity to align motivations, creating a win-win between you and your key personnel. It's a politically correct solution with a simple concept everyone can get behind it: "if we make more money, I'll share it with you." A carrot-and-stick approach, go get it!

Powerful! Especially as society wants to see a greater distribution of wealth from the top, a profit-sharing plan seems to strike the chord of the perfect way to incentivize key people. So, does it work?

The reality of a profit-sharing plan is that it can be more harmful than the incentives we were hoping it would create. Like the other forms of remuneration discussed, the good intentions of this pillar are there. But once again, the key employee is left with promises but little control.

The main violation here comes from one of the questions of *Intuitive Compensation,* "Under this plan is there a scenario where they can get nothing?"

A bad year for your company, which may not necessarily be a bad year for your key person's, could leave them receiving no profits. Nothing. And considering a bad year is when you need them the most, the promise of 'nothing' is not much incentive to work off of. A profit-sharing plan that doesn't pay out during a difficult year could compound your problems during tough times.

Not only that, even during good years business owners simply aren't aware of what's actually at stake in a profit-sharing plan. With the concept being easy to get behind, owners tend to structure it as a reward that should be welcomed with open arms. It is also the hope that the arrangement will strengthen the relationship between owner and employee as well.

Believe it or not, profit sharing plans could be seen as the poster child for the "what can go wrong, will go wrong" with *employee math*. The blind side comes as a profit-sharing plan may completely change the mindset of the employee, how he sees you as a leader, and how he feels about the decisions being made by the company.

Once **profits** become the meter that determines the resulting reward, you have inadvertently created an environment where your key people nitpick every decision you make that could affect profits (their reward). The more "profits" they make you, the more likely you are to spend, to expand or reduce taxes. You've left yourself wide open to upset your key player.

When it comes to best practices, at least some portion of your business decisions should be separate from their incentive system. Combining the two violates *Intuitive Compensation* insights by not separating their wealth and retention strategy from the business.

Invest in a new marketing strategy, upgrade to first class on a flight, or hire a new employee. **ALL** of your business decisions impact the profits that will flow through to their pocket. Do you see how you changed your relationship? The smaller the business, the more impact these decisions will have on the bottom line.

Here's the catch. If a key person is not happy with your profit-sharing plan, they will most likely not be good at communicating their concerns with you. Instead, this Pillar could light a fire inside of them for change. When they feel change represents a path forward for them, they most likely will not communicate these feelings or intentions with you.

This person is now a sleeper inside your business that can hurt your culture and steal inside information from you. Once the idea of change is planted in the mind of a key employee it's hard to stop it from spreading. If this happens, without a strong enough *retention compensation* package in place, offering *more* is no longer a driver for them. Their only cure becomes *change*.

5ᵀᴴ PILLAR: THE PILLAR OF "LAWYERING"

"It's like you own it... but you don't actually own it."
Same pig, different shade of lipstick."
- Kevin D. Monaghan

Options such as phantom stock, restricted stock units, alternate share classes, profits interest, and stock appreciation rights all reside in the home of the Fifth Pillar. This is a new age pillar of compensation and I refer to it as the "Pillar of Lawyering."

When business owners realized they needed a way to reduce the downside of equity and profit-sharing plans they turned to legal counsel to avoid the pitfalls of the previous pillars.

This pillar exploded in popularity hitting an exposed nerve with owners because it provides protections to businesses in case things don't work out with their key players.

Private equity and venture capital companies have played a big role in turning these concepts mainstream, causing these tactics to trickle down to the smallest of start-ups seeking relief from having given away too much equity or profits early on.

Does it work?

At first, there was a lot of success in using this pillar. But it didn't take long for the downside of "Lawyering" to start raising warning flags for everyone. It turned out the Fifth Pillar left out two very important players in its goal of achieving retention and a win/win situation: The key employee and the potential buyer.

Let's take phantom stock for example. Phantom stock is probably the single best motivator in the build-to-sell a business model for key employees. Phantom stock is simply a promise to pay a bonus in the form of either the value of company shares, or the increase in that value over a period of time.

Phantom stock needs a triggering event for an employee to get paid, for example, the sale of the company. This would in turn pay out a lump sum as if the key employee (the holder of the phantom shares) owned an actual percentage of the company, hence, the reason why it caught fire with private equity firms. "It's like you own it, but you don't actually own it." If the key person leaves, or the company doesn't sell, then they get nothing. Tsk, Tsk.

For businesses where the key employees are expendable in an exit sale, phantom stock might be the best way to go. Phantom stock would give key players a slice of the sale price. These opportunities would include businesses that revolve around software, pure customer acquisitions, or any business where *people* aren't going to be important to the purchasing company.

But for most businesses it's the people, namely key employees, who make all the difference in getting a high multiple in a sale. Would you buy a company where the top two salespeople, who represented 70% of revenues, had nothing in place to retain them? Securing revenue and growth in a firm is what the buyer is interested in, not buying a job or a risk.

Buyers are now savvy enough to know that buying a company where employees own phantom stock is like buying a company where everyone has just hit the lotto. On their dime! When a buyer triggers a phantom stock payout for key employees, this could provide them with startup money for their own firm, a career change or a much-needed sabbatical; all reasons they would leave.

Rounding out the other common options:

1. Restricted stock: refers to unregistered *shares* of ownership in a corporation that are issued to corporate affiliates, such as executives and directors. In other words, ownership with vesting and a lot of rules around the shares, winds up being "like equity, with less rights." When the key person leaves you risk losing the revenue they were producing and now adding an expense because you have to buy those shares back. Double whammy if they leave.

2. Alternate share classes include non-voting shares, redeemable shares, management shares, alphabet shares and deferred shares are a version of ownership that provides the "feel" of ownership, but still restrict your rights versus actually owning outright the common voting stock. Same pig, different lipstick.

3. Stock appreciation rights (SARS) and profits interests (PI) are excel sheet, I.Q. darlings. Each represents a committment, usually a balance sheet formula, for an

executive to be rewarded for their help in growing the company above it's current share price (SARS) or above it's current profit levels (PI) as of today. Commonly utilized when hiring outside talent, it's a way to reward executives for the future, without rewarding them for what's already been established and achieved in the past. Both eventually wind up with all the same problems of equity or a profit-sharing plan. Fighting over valuation levels and who ultimately gets to decide what money flows through to the value of the shares (SARS), or the profits (PI), are the downsides.

I always ask people who are offering restricted stock units, SARS, different share classes, or profits interest, if they've ever owned these structures for themselves? Outside of phantom stock, which is usually accompanied by a negative experience, the answer is almost always, "no."

CHAPTER EIGHT, PART I:
THE TOOL... OF THE SIXTH PILLAR

*"Playing the piano is easy, once you get it...
Such is that of the Sixth Pillar"*
- Kevin D. Monaghan

The Sixth Pillar combines the goals of a key person with <u>retention</u>. These strategies associated with the Sixth Pillars have names such as 162 Leverage Executive Bonus, Split-Dollar, Restricted Property Trusts, Executive Bonus, Double Bonus, ESOP, Restricted Bonus, SERP's and many more.

I refer to the strategies of the Sixth Pillar as the "Pillar of Complexity" as these strategies can seem a bit overwhelming at first. Not to worry, this chapter will help you understand the high-level concept behind *how* they work. To illustrate my point, I will turn to a story about the nostalgic lemonade stand.

Daniel, Ryan and Stacy grew up in the suburbs of Upstate New York. Like many siblings, they were competitive over everything. For the brothers that meant being competitive in sports, video games, grades, saving money and teasing their sister.

In their small town nothing went unnoticed. When the neighbors were moving out and their lemonade stand was up for sale, Daniel and Ryan jumped at the opportunity.

You should know this lemonade stand was the pride of the neighborhood. Parents and children alike never hesitated to pay for a tall glass of lemonade on a hot summer day. For the young entrepreneurs it was a sure bet.

Daniel quickly assumed leadership of the lemonade stand, claiming it was his right as the oldest child, because, well, that's just the way it is.

Naturally, when we have success as an owner the green monster of envy can make that success feel unfair to others, and Ryan instantly felt jealous.

Nonetheless, the brothers were excited to have the lemonade stand and agreed on one thing, their sister Stacy would have nothing to do with it.

Daniel assigned Ryan the job of running the stand and making the lemonade while Daniel would go around the neighborhood and get kids to come over and play. They settled on a wage and began selling lemonade.

Success came quickly and the lemonade stand was a hit.

But as Ryan slaved over the juicer under the hot summer sun, and missed out on all the fun the other neighborhood kids were having, he became increasingly frustrated. Until finally he marched up to Daniel and demanded he pay him more money or he would stop working the stand.

Now, when you're a child, management is easy and Daniel took matters into his own hands.

But even as a child this management style can get you into trouble.

It was time for mom and dad to step in.

After dad gave everyone a thorough "talking to," mom came up with a plan. She knew Daniel loved being in control and Ryan was a workhorse who sometimes underestimated his own value. So she invented what she coined the "Lunchbox Loot."

Every day after they counted their earnings, Daniel would put $5 into a lunchbox that the brothers would keep in their parent's room. Business would run as normal. Daniel, as the owner, would continue to pocket the profits after expenses and Ryan would remain working the booth and earning his salary.

The only difference was if Ryan kept working, and did a good job, he would get to take away the lunchbox at the end of the season. If he didn't, only half of the lunchbox loot would go to Ryan and the other, back to Daniel.

It was a plan that everyone was happy with (except Stacy) and the very popular lemonade stand remained fully functioning until it was time to go back to school.

* * *

Fast forward to today where everyone is a working adult.

Daniel owns a company with his brother Ryan as his key employee. Their childhood lemonade stand has grown into the region's first fresh juice delivery hub. The business is thriving and making more money than anyone could have ever imagined from when they were boys. That being said, frustrations loom over what will happen next.

Ryan is again feeling underwhelmed by his salary and is entertaining offers from competitors. He's even looked into starting his own juice distribution service.

At the same time Daniel has received offers to buy his company, but hasn't shared with Ryan that any of this was happening.

Their success had led to the beginnings of an underlying tension between the two brothers. Daniel noticed Ryan acting differently and was making subtle comments here and there which implied he should have *more*.

Daniel wanted to find a solution that removed this grey cloud of tension from their relationship so the business could move forward as usual. Trying to "do right" while at the same time navigating his interests, the business's best interests, and his brother's potentials in life, was not going to be easy.

Daniel thought back to the early days and the "lunchbox loot" strategy. If it worked before, could it work again? Daniel laid out all his options for compensation:

1) Pay more
2) Benefits
3) Equity
4) Profit share
5) Phantom stock
6) Bucket story

For Ryan, the emotions of *employee math* poked questions and concerns such as:

I Tool

1) What's in it for me?

2) Your indecision is my frustration

3) Clarity + Control

4) Time is my favorite asset

Daniel remembered how mom had worked to help his brother and himself come to a solution that gave them both clarity at the end of each summer. Daniel again called in third parties to help him see if an adulthood version of "lunchbox loot" could be recreated. Mom and dad are now replaced by professionals.

(actual facial expressions and comments may vary)

Daniel was making $600,000 per year in profit from the juice business. Not being able to see the books, Ryan on the other hand, only had a rough estimate of what the actual profits were but as *employee math* does, he was over estimating it. Another thing *employee math* does is it discounts the actual time, risk, costs and investments that were needed to keep running the business and get it to a profitable place. These factors weighed on Ryan and caused him to see his brother, Daniel, as greedy.

With the third party in place, a plan was laid out that would require Daniel to put $100,000 in the "lunchbox" or, from here on out, what we will refer to as a "**bucket**."

The large sum of $100,000 made Daniel a bit nervous, so they structured it as $50,000 constituting the owner's base level of commitment to the program, and $50,000 as a flexible amount. This way, if there was a recession, or bad year of business, Daniel had some flexibility and breathing room.

Daniel agreed to bring Ryan into the process. But before presenting a solution, it's important to see where Ryan is emotionally and if he's in the mindset to be retained. Too many people jump right into presenting to the key person (I.Q., Intelligence Quotient), because they become sold on the fact that it's a great idea. *Intuitive Compensation* knows the importance of taking a few extra steps to make sure Ryan is appreciated, retainable and treated like an equal (all E.Q. items). Going this "extra mile" also gives the owner an opportunity to identify any issue and squash it. If you're going to commit to *more,* you want your relationship to have the best chance of keeping the grey clouds of tension away.

Working with professionals, the brothers were able to get their bucket strategy in place, giving everyone clarity on what's in it for them. If a problem comes up, they'd all know where they stand at any given moment. Just as it had in the past, the adult version of "lunchbox loot" allowed Daniel to commit *more* to his brother than he would have otherwise. Both understand and have clarity around the exchange of *more* for *retention.*

In real life these "buckets" are used all around us. Take the national example of Jim Harbaugh and the University of Michigan. Jim had a typical key-employee-journey. He went to the San Francisco 49ers and gave them two playoff berths after more than a decade without a winning season. Like any top performer, he was quickly receiving offers from competitors. The University of Michigan wound up signing him, and they made sure to use the Sixth Pillar to keep him.

"I don't think about it," Jim Harbaugh said, when asked how he turned the losing NCAA team around so quickly. "See if we can't be better today than we were yesterday. See if we can't be better tomorrow than we were today."[24] Words to live by.

How great would it be to do our jobs with only the thought of making our products better than they were yesterday? Alas, as business owners we are subject to day to day affairs such as salaries, taxes, social and emotional welfare of employees, loans and so forth, that sometimes leave our growth plans on the back burner.

It could be argued that Jim Harbaugh was able to give the answer he did for one really good reason; as the head coach for the Michigan Wolverines, he brings in an astounding $7.5 million dollars annually. Of that amount, $2 million goes into his "bucket." By using the Sixth Pillar, the University has made him one of the highest paid coaches in college football.

---

[24] Ivan Maisel, "How Jim Harbaugh Made Michigan So Good So Fast," ESPN, October 16, 2015, https://www.espn.com/college-football/story/_/id/13893353/how-michigan-wolverines-got-good-fast-jim-harbaugh

But it doesn't stop there. The Sixth Pillar allowed the University of Michigan to have an abundant mindset with their key person, while at the same time, fulfilling their own *best interests*. It was a no-brainer for the University of Michigan board to say "yes," because they structured the "bucket" where they would be able to recoup all, or at least a significant portion, of the money allocated to Harbaugh if he left.

How is this possible? This is the power of the Sixth Pillar. Cost recovery, with interest. Protection if a key person leaves. This is just a taste of the impact and potential the Sixth Pillar of compensation brings to the table.

The downside to this pillar is that it takes patience and education to understand. In fact, it took some time, but other Universities are starting to get it and implement "buckets" with their coaches. For example, Dabo Swinney of Clemson and Dawn Staley of University of South Carolina now have their own "buckets."

Once "in-the-know" you'll see the Sixth Pillar being used all around us and you'll start to see how:

- University's use it with their coaches, one of the ultimate win-wins.
- Non-Profits and Credit Unions use these concepts to retain talent and compete with the private sector.[25]

---

[25] Pesh, John. "Why Split-Dollar Life Insurance Is Gaining Popularity." August 5, 2019. https://www.cumanagement.com/articles/2019/08/why-split-dollar-life-insurance-gaining-popularity

- Hospitals use it to keep doctors, especially those seeking to save on excise taxes paying specialist doctors with salaries over $1m.
- Multi-generational businesses use it to keep the peace, transfer ownership, or equalize the estate.
- Businesses seeking on-boarding new partners and/or exiting older partners.
- Fortune 500 companies use it with their employees.[26]
- Businesses use it to fund their pension obligations efficiently.
- Owners with no plan use it to keep their options open while retaining their key people in the meantime.
- Partnerships use it to keep their friendships intact as their performance skews from their equity split ratios.
- Minority owned, Veteran owned, and licensed professionals use it to keep their key people and keep their "owned" status.
- Private Equity and Investment Bankers use these strategies to gain an edge and lower their risk when buying companies.

The list goes on.

This pillar even gives the hardheaded owner, who everyone knows is struggling with a way to give up control, the

---

[26] Schultz, Ellen E. and Theo Francis. "How Life Insurance Morphed Into a Corporate Finance Tool." December 30, 2002.
https://online.wsj.com/public/resources/documents/dec_30_one.htm

courage to start taking steps to plan for the inevitable "exit plan." At the same time the owner can maintain control and reserve their right to change course as they see fit, the key employee can have their clarity.

The strategies associated with the Sixth Pillar of compensation could give business owners an edge. You'll see how it allows organizations to commit more than they thought possible, enabling their key person to feel like a Producer or Legend in their own right... in exchange for retention.

CHAPTER EIGHT, PART II:
THE TOOL... WHAT IS THE BUCKET?

"The greatest hero, is often the person you least expect."
- Kevin D. Monaghan

Hollywood movies greatest thrills come when a surprise twist reveals itself at the end, like in M. Night Shyamalan's *'The Sixth Sense'* with the famous line "I see dead people."[27] When you realize the protagonist Bruce Willis was one of the dead himself, it suddenly becomes so obvious. *How did I miss that!?* you think to yourself.

When we look at the "twist" or the "hero" of the bucket it also comes with a surprise ending. In fact, I'd argue that the reason more people don't know about the Sixth Pillar, is because they give up before they even get started.

Technically, almost any asset class can be used as the "bucket." Equity, stocks, bank savings account, property, the company itself, a bitcoin account, just to name a few. But time and again, the "twist" is that the bucket is usually made of specifically tailored cash value life insurance policies.

Dabo Swinney, Jim Harbaugh, boards of directors, business owners and key employees all at some point skeptically asked,

---

[27] *The Sixth Sense*, directed by M. Night Shyamalan (1999; Philadelphia, PA: Buena Vista Pictures, 2000), DVD.

"why cash value life insurance?" Just like in the movies, once you understand the reasons why an organization would use life insurance, it becomes obvious.

For the same reasons cash value life insurance policies were used for Jim Harbaugh's and Dabo Swinney's (who recently signed a 10-year, $93 million contract)[28] compensation package, you should consider it too.

The reasons one would use cash value life insurance as the tool of the Sixth Pillar:

First: If the employee you retain becomes disabled, and the disability waiver of premium was selected, the insurance company could continue filling up the bucket. No other pillar covers disability so effectively, and no other asset class transfers this risk so clearly. Salary, profit share, etc. would all come to an end in the event of a disability if the key person could no longer work.

---

28 Gene Sapakoff, "Dabo Swinney gets record $93 dollar contract at Clemson, new Alabama buyout terms," Post and Courier, April 26, 2019, www.postandcourier.com/columnists/dabo-swinney-gets-record-million-contract-at-clemson-new-alabama/article_8bf61320-6833-11e9-bfb2-eba9dc3741fa.html

Second: If the employee you wish to retain passes away, the insurance company will fill up the bucket and write a check to his surviving family members. Depending on the structure it could also act as key person insurance. Life insurance proceeds are generally received income tax free.

Third: Depending on the structure used, the cash value of the life insurance policy could be protected from certain creditors. For example, with an Executive Bonus Plan, if the business gets in trouble financially then the key employee's portion of the bucket would be protected from creditors (but not necessaritly from the employee's personal creditors). With another structure, let's say Endoresement Split Dollar, if your key person becomes bankrupt, the policy owned by the business would not usually be part of the bankruptcy proceeding. Not all structures will provide this protection, and each state has differet laws that would apply, but seeking this type of protection could be a sticking point for some key employee's (or businesses) when finalizing the plan.

Fourth: Cash value inside a life insurance policy grows tax deferred. Which means as your retained employee makes more money, they won't be subject to taxation on the growth inside the policy. A lower annual tax burden and a tax-deferred vehicle over the long term will compound their wealth, and compound your retention strategy. Hold the bucket long enough, you could even access the cash values without income or capital gains taxes. Note, however, that policy loans will reduce the cash value and death benefit of the policy.

Fifth: Let the business be the risk, **_NOT_** your compensation plan. _Intuitive compensation_ knows that an incentive that could result in receiving "nothing" can backfire on you and cause your key person to leave. The specific types of insurance we would use would have guarantees around the cash value and the growth.

Sixth: Collateral. Because cash value whole life insurance is so commonly used as the asset class for these structures, life companies are already set up to act like "lunch box loot" where we used mom's room to hold the funds. Meaning, your key employee can't just run off with the bucket.

CHAPTER EIGHT, PART III:
THE TOOL... OF AN ABUNDANT MINDSET

"If Culture is King, then Clarity is Queen...
Long live the Queen!"
- Kevin D. Monaghan

Now that you know what the Sixth Pillar of Compensation is and how it could help you retain your key employee, it's time to ask the question from the business owner's perspective: "What's in it for me?"

If you're going to create an abundant mindset with your compensation strategy and offer *more* to your key person, then it would behoove you to position yourself better too. Afterall, it's much easier to commit our hard earned dollars to something that helps us make money.

Whether you plan to continue running your business, sell it, or wind up transferring it for lack of a more creative exit, a "bucket" strategy must meet the needs of everyone. Not only that, it must meet the needs of everyone regardless of what exit strategy ultimately has you departing from the business.

As an owner, your choices are few:

1. <u>Sell it:</u> We all dream of exiting our business with a windfall sale. Reality doesn't always play out that way. According to BizBuySell.com, in 2018 there were 10,312 business transactions for an average exit of

$275,000[29]. That is hardly enough money to recreate the income the business was generating.

    a. Positive: A windfall sale leaves you free and clear of the business.

    b. Negative: Your business may have been able to produce a better return on your money than what you invest your lump sum in. And, what do you do with your life now?

2. **Wait & See:** This means you don't really have a plan, so you keep running your business. You have no plan except committing to thinking about it *more*. Meaning you either own it until you pass away, gift it "one day," or "do something" later.

    a. Positive: You stay in control.

    b. Negative: The key employee begins loathing you for the lack of clarity around what's in it for them. This is the one key people despise the most.

3. **Transfer #1 Self-Financing Note:** In this case, you're using some form of your own cash flow to purchase yourself out. This is the harsh reality of how most small businesses will pass. Because the economics aren't

---

[29] Michale Guta, "Number of Businesses Bought and Sold Hit Record Level in 2018," BizBuySell, Jan 27, 2019, https://smallbiztrends.com/2019/01/bizbuysell-annual-2018-insight-report.html

great when you're buying yourself out with what's already yours, it is also the main reason so many default to the Wait & See plan. Reality is, it's normally more profitable to keep running the company than to have employees buy you out.

    a. <u>Positive</u>: They get to become an owner. S-Corps mean K-1's.

    b. <u>Negative:</u> Loans, no control, maybe using your own money to buy yourself out? As a minority shareholder, you don't really have any control and the leverage taking out loans creates could cause stress in the owner – borrower relationship.

4. <u>Transfer #2 Sinking Fund:</u> Enter the Sixth Pillar. The same retention plan can be used to solve the key employee's biggest problem. They have no money.

    a. <u>Positive:</u> You maintain control, and the "bucket" incentivizes retention while simultaneously builds up their sinking fund.

    b. <u>Negative:</u> Free will. They can still leave or in the future, or they may decide they don't want to own the business anymore. On the positive, this may then leave you with a BIG golden handcuff on them which may be good news for your retirement.

With the number of business owners in their 50's and 60's with no clarity on a succession plan in place, younger key people leave fearing becoming stuck as a Hustler well into <u>your</u> retirement. An aging owner with a younger protégé or child in the business, can leave them in the ultimate state of frustration. Wondering.

By positioning your key employee/s with a "bucket" strategy, the money you allocate for retention could later be used to begin buying you out. This way they are not becoming frustrated wondering what your plans are without reward. They have their own clarity on what's in it for them, and they too have a choice in the future.

All that being said, at some point you will see the need to explore your options and a potential exit plan. When coming in for a landing with your business exit, retention and the Sixth Pillar could be the firm runway that guides you in.[30][31]

---

[30] Pesh, John. "Why Split-Dollar Life Insurance Is Gaining Popularity." August 5, 2019. https://www.cumanagement.com/articles/2019/08/why-split-dollar-life-insurance-gaining-popularity

[31] See Disclaimer Page

CHAPTER NINE:
YOUR BUCKET

"If you pick the right people and give them the opportunity to spread their wings and put compensation as a carrier behind it you almost don't have to manage them."
- Jack Welch

A good business owner knows that Intuitive Compensation will first consider the profitability of structuring a retention plan before diving in. They'll consider structures that allow them to deduct the amount they put into the "bucket" and turn to owner math to develop the most worthwhile strategy.

A "bucket" takes any compensation plan and turns it into a powerful retention tool. To the owner, the formula for its success would look something like this:

Cost of Turnover > Cost of Bucket = Profitable Strategy

The "cost of turnover" is not only costly in time and revenue, it can be emotionally draining as well. An ill-timed departure can stall growth plans, lead to others leaving, or have us doing the Hustler activities we've grown to loathe.

Each business will have its own break-even time frame when developing key people, but for most businesses it will take a few years to recoup the investment of developing a new person in the first place. Whether your curve is shorter or longer, the curve looks something like this:

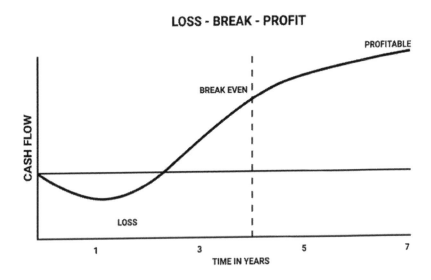

Regardless of how quickly you break even in your business with a new hire, it helps if they can stay while keeping the profits coming in.

Let's take a look at how implementing a "bucket" strategy could impact the bottom line. As an example, we'll use Dr. Paul's dental office with his new associate dentist, right out of school, Sarah. At the end of this book you can review a more detailed version of this scenario in a case study, but for now, know that Dr. Paul wants to reduce turnover and Sarah wants to get rid of her student loans.

If we calculate the simple revenue and profit numbers with turnover, the breakeven of the *owner math* would look something like this:

With Turnover: Losing Dental Associate Every 3 Years:

	Revenue	Profit
Year 1	300	(100k)
Year 2	500	100
Year 3	650	250
Year 4	300	(100k)
Year 5	500	100
Total	2.9m	500k

If Dr. Paul aims to reduce turnover, he needs to explore solutions where both he and Sarah can meet their interests by working together. A successful bucket strategy could help both parties achieve what they want, and help the bottom line at the same time. A so called win-win:

Retention: Keeping Dental Associate 6 Years:

	Rev. w/Sarah	Profit	Bucket	Tax benefit	Lower Pay
Year 1	300k	(100k)	60k		25k
Year 2	500k	100	60k		25k
Year 3	650k	250	60k		25k
Year 4	650k	250	60k		25k
Year 5	650k	250	60k		25k
Year 6	650k	250	60k		25k
Total	3.4m	1m	360k	122k	150k

Taking all the factors into play:

(Bucket Cost)	360k
Tax Deduction Year 6	(122k)
Salary Reduction	(150k)
Net Bucket Cost	88k

Armed with the knowledge that turnover could cost Dr. Paul over $500,000 in profits, as opposed to a mere net risk of $88,000 if Sarah fulfills her full six years, it was a no-brainer for him to commit to a "bucket" for Sarah. Working together with a third party Dr. Paul would utilize a bucket strategy which he would contribute *more* money overall to a "bucket" that would accumulate funds toward Sarah's loans in exchange for her retention. (See Case Study in Chapter 10)

Dr. Paul profits + Sarah Pays Off School Debt = 7yr. win-win

With the math behind you it now comes to the design phase of how you can structure your "bucket." The nice part about non-qualified compensation options is the flexibility to hone-in on the key employees specific goals, treating them like a Producer or Legend right within your business.

When it comes to the structure of "buckets" there are three high level ways to think about it: A bonus bucket, splitting the bucket or loaning you a bucket.

BONUS

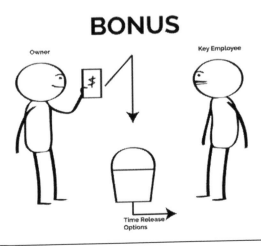

Bonusing options when it comes to the Sixth Pillar are varied. Strategies like Executive Bonus, Double Bonus, Restricted Bonus and other designs where the company can fill up a "bucket" and bonus it now or later. With these structures an owner is typically seeking some form of tax deduction. When it comes to these bonus strategies, the biggest determination is time. Most bonus strategies are implemented by contributing to the bucket monthly or annually, and as time goes on, the accumulation continues to crescendo. It's hard to walk away from someone filling up a bucket for you. Other bonus structures, such as Restricted Bonus, seeks to delay the release of the bucket to the key employee until later.

Next, we have lending:

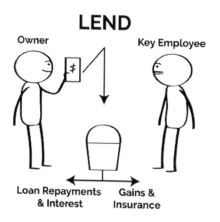

LEND

Owner   Key Employee

Loan Repayments   Gains &
& Interest   Insurance

Sometimes, instead of paying into the bucket for the benefit of the employee, we look to use leverage and <u>lend</u> them the money for the bucket instead of bonusing it. By lending, you may not get a tax deduction, but you maintain a lot of control. In this scenario the benefits take longer to play out but it's much easier to commit *more* when we know our money will eventually be returned with interest. This is similar to the solution the universities used with the college coaches. The key employee in these structures typically stays or intends to stay 10 years or longer. CEO's, C-level executives, non-profits, credit unions, private businesses, families, and more are the typical users of these structures.

Finally we have scenarios where we split the bucket.

SPLIT

Splitting the bucket is implemented in strategies like the 162 Leverage Executive Bonus plan. It's like having your cake and eating it too. You can explore getting a deduction and maintain some control over the bucket as there are elements both of bonus and loan with this plan. Each participant knows what portion of the bucket is theirs and has clarity over their portion. This was the concept behind "lunch box loot" where the brothers split the bucket and mom oversaw the rules of the bucket.

"Buckets" come in all shapes and sizes. So do key employees. Now that you know the Six Pillars of compensation that outline your choices, and understand how the insights of *Intuitive Compensation* may help you craft your strategy, what will your next compensation move be?...

What could a "bucket" do for you?

Want Our Help Designing Your Bucket?

Get on Our Schedule & Tell Us Your Story

Call (877) 70-LEARN -

(877) 705-3276

Or via web by going to

www.intuitivecompensation.com

What to Expect:

Get on our schedule above.

Tell us Your Story over a 30 minute call.

If we can help, we'll get to work on concepts and ideas.

Set up virtual meeting to review "bucket" ideas with you.

CHAPTER TEN:
CASE STUDY

"Money does not solve people's problems,
so allocate towards their goals instead of their pockets."
- Kevin D. Monaghan

ICG CASE STUDY #1 –
PAUL'S DENTAL PRACTICE

Situation:

Paul runs a successful dental practice in Albany, New York. He has been the sole practitioner and owner of his operation for over 29 years. After decades of tirelessly long hours, work-related issues in the form of streaking back pains and aching fingers have surfaced. Paul is ready for a change but one that does not take away from the comfortable lifestyle he has created for himself and his family.

Critical Issue:

A decade ago, Paul took on an office expansion project that led to the hiring of two young dentists. The team grew and the increase in revenue led to a major shift in his business approach. He became an owner, and what we call at Intuitive Compensation Group (ICG) a Producer (see chapter 3). Paul was now setting his sights on 'Legend' status and decided to go into another expansion that would scale his business and extend out of town. The proposed plan for his two key dentists was to buy into the expansion with loans that would be paid off as profits increased. The profit sharing plan he designed did not however, address the issues of *how* profits would be calculated and what control the dentists would have over that allocation. Furthermore, as the two dentists under Paul grew more experienced and developed a client base, they wanted to know how the expansion would benefit them in the advancement of their careers. This uncertainty in both IQ and EQ of Paul's key people, led them to leave and start their own business elsewhere. Paul has now had to backtrack his business development plans.

Strategy Formulation:

Paul came to Intuitive Compensation Group for a solution to his problem. The scaling of his business was still his main objective but he wants to be sure he is planning for the future when it comes to his greatest asset in this expansion, his key employees. After searching through many resumes, he was able to narrow his ideal candidates to two. With ICG's instructions on hand, he gave himself a guideline for the questions he would ask during the interview. These were the results of those interviews:

Sarah, was in her mid-thirties and wanted to start a family sooner rather than later. One of her and her husband's major concerns however, is their combined student debt which extends well into the $200,000 range. Sarah tested as a strong fit with the firm's culture and her personality profile indicated she was a team player. She was well-received by the interview team.

Kim, who was also in her mid-thirties, was single and had no plans to get married. She tested well culturally and in her ability to lead. Kim was entrepreneurial in nature and talked about equity in her interview. She also mentioned not wanting to take out any loans. Paul liked her, but had some concerns about his business taking a backseat to her ambition and potentially subjecting himself to a repeat of past events where his key employee left.

Areas of Consideration

We asked Paul to put himself in the shoes of a potential dental associate and what they are likely seeking:

Dentist	Dental Associate Retention
1. Avoid buybacks for departing dentist.	1. Provide Clarity.
2. Yes to bonus incentive structure, No to equity.	2. Don't want buy in.
	3. Make an exit, clean and easy.
3. Lead and Help the associate.	4. Avoid loans.
4. Focus on being more profitable, with less conflict of interest.	5. Don't want to be punished for growing the business.

We Provided:

Based on Paul's input, we came up with some concepts for him that we believed represented a possible solution. With

Sarah, we naturally looked into creating a student debt program. We also wanted any solution to promote family as this was clearly stated as one of her plans for the near future, it would only be wise to include this in a retention plan. Sarah was asking for a starting salary of $175,000 for the first year. This was viable for the company but what Paul wanted to know was the retention outlook for his potential employee.

Here was the concept we came up with, which is known as a 162 Leveraged Executive Bonus as we discussed in Chapter 9.

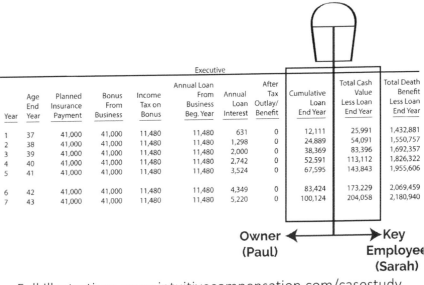

					Executive					
Year	Age End Year	Planned Insurance Payment	Bonus From Business	Income Tax on Bonus	Annual Loan From Business Beg. Year	Annual Loan Interest	After Tax Outlay/ Benefit	Cumulative Loan End Year	Total Cash Value Less Loan End Year	Total Death Benefit Less Loan End Year
1	37	41,000	41,000	11,480	11,480	631	0	12,111	25,991	1,432,881
2	38	41,000	41,000	11,480	11,480	1,298	0	24,889	54,091	1,550,757
3	39	41,000	41,000	11,480	11,480	2,000	0	38,369	83,396	1,692,357
4	40	41,000	41,000	11,480	11,480	2,742	0	52,591	113,112	1,826,322
5	41	41,000	41,000	11,480	11,480	3,524	0	67,595	143,843	1,955,606
6	42	41,000	41,000	11,480	11,480	4,349	0	83,424	173,229	2,069,459
7	43	41,000	41,000	11,480	11,480	5,220	0	100,124	204,058	2,180,940

Owner (Paul) ← → Key Employee (Sarah)

Full Illustration: www.intuitivecompensation.com/casestudy

In the bucket structure illustrated above, the right side of the bucket would belong to Sarah while the left to Paul. As you can see, by year five, there would be enough funds in her side of the bucket to cover a large chunk of her student loans. If she stayed on for seven years, she would have enough to pay off her entire debt. During these years, Paul could also choose to bonus his side of the bucket to her.

Result:

Before going over any numbers with Sarah we gathered some more information from her. As it happened, Sarah's loans were tied to her income which meant that any additional income she reported would increase her amount due on the loans each month. This was a major stressor and would do some damage to her situation. She also had a high interest rate on the loan so as it matured, the initial proposed plan would not be enough to pay off her debt.

Working together with the best interest of both sides in mind, we came up with a solution. Sarah agreed to a base salary of $150,000 with $5000 per month going into her bucket from the employer's side.

The version below is one way a Split Dollar plan can be structured:

		Employee					Employer		
Age End Year	Imputed Income	Before-Tax Outlay Beg Year+	After-Tax Outlay Beg Year+	Net Cash Surrender Value End Year	Net Death Beneath End Year	Before-Tax Outlay Beg Year +	After-Tax Outlay Beg Year+	Net Cash Surrender Value End Year	Net Death Beneath End Year
38	427	0	119	0	1,523,749	60,000	60,000	53,749	60,000
39	467	0	131	0	1,609,560	60,000	60,000	111,435	120,000
40	533	0	149	0	1,718,510	60,000	60,000	171,867	180,000
41	619	0	173	0	1,820,309	60,000	60,000	233,990	240,000
42	691	0	193	0	1,918,863	60,000	60,000	298,744	300,000
43	780	0	218	0	1,999,886	60,000	60,000	363,048	363,048
44		-101,654	0	266,071	1,933,659	0	-122,400	0	0

www.intuitivecompensation.com/casestudy

From Paul's perspective, this plan committed a little bit more, but he could recoup that $5000 per month if Sarah left before six years. He could commit to more, because this allowed him to net less out of pocket than he would get back if he simply paid her $175,000.

For Sarah the plan was a hit. Not only would she have a clear vision for the repayment of her debt in a matter of six years, she would also have peace of mind knowing her soon-to-be family would have a life insurance benefit of over $1.5M if anything happened to her.

When we caught up with Sarah, she was thriving in her work and was getting exactly what she wanted. Paul is looking into structuring a new bucket, as she plans to continue to stay on after she pays off her debt.

Next, Paul had to learn about Kim's needs and how to develop a plan that worked for her tenure with his company. Right off the bat we could tell that Kim was every bit as ambitious as Paul had mentioned, if not more.

With Kim we implemented the 162 Leverage Executive Bonus with a twist...

						Executive			
Year	Age End Year	Planned Insurance Payment	Bonus From Business	Income Tax on Bonus	Annual Loan From Business Beg. year	Annual Loan Interest	After Tax Outlay/ Benefit	Cummulative Loan End Year	Total Cash Value Less Loan End year	Total Death Benefit Less Loan End Year
1	37	41,000	41,000	11,480	11,480	631	0	12,111	26,189	1,198,70
2	38	41,000	41,000	11,480	11,480	1,298	0	24,889	54,538	1,291,82
3	39	41,000	41,000	11,480	11,480	2,000	0	38,369	84,132	1,401,50
4	40	41,000	41,000	11,480	11,480	2,742	0	52,591	114,180	1,505,18
5	41	41,000	41,000	11,480	11,480	3,524	0	67,595	145,301	1,605,45
6	42	41,000	41,000	11,480	11,480	4,349	0	83,424	175,270	1,694,14
7	43	41,000	41,000	11,480	11,480	5,220	0	100,124	206,754	1,781,77

www.intuitivecompensation.com/casestudy

In addition to the 162 Leverage Executive Bonus plan, Paul added a stock option for her to become partner. This meant that at year 5 there will be over $200,000 in cash value in their shared bucket. At the end of the five years, she could exchange her portion (exercise her stock option) of the cash value in the bucket for 10% of the company.

This is a powerful tool that can delay or position equity conversations, even avert them all together. Unlike a loan, earn in, or restricted stock units, this plan changes the psyche of becoming an equity holder. It is one thing to say yes to shares when your cash flow is providing them everything anyways, it's another thing when, such as in this example, they have to take money that is already IN THEIR HANDS and exchange it for a minority share of your company. It completely changes how they think about the decision to own a part of your company. Not only that, but Paul has time and options, including making her a counter offer if he doesn't want her to buy in.

Kim hadn't heard of this before but she understood right away how it would benefit her. She had a path forward that would give her options while building wealth. She also really liked that the stock option was locked in, so if she helped build the company's wealth, she wasn't going to be punished if she chose to exchange equity.

From Paul's point of view, he was used to giving away equity upfront, having time to build a relationship with Kim seemed fair to him. In addition, he had some protections in place if she left. Not having to buy back equity upon departure was a huge win for him.

For a more details:

1. The exhibit on the next pages in this book.
2. For supporting illustrations, please visit:
   www.intuitivecompensation.com/casestudy

ICG CASE STUDY #2 –
CEO & LEADERSHIP TEAM

Situation:

A hospital registered as a non-profit was looking to expand throughout the Mid-Atlantic. In order to keep the cash flow coming in to help fund the expansion, the board of directors needed to retain the physicians at their current locations. Additionally, they needed to formulate a plan to retain the new and existing key physicians for the newly acquired hospitals.

Critical Issue:

With growth, comes challenges. At the time we met, the board was dealing with 30+ physicians who had just left to start their own medical group. Current physicians were leaving, citing they felt less appreciated in a bigger organization. Physician turnover was causing problems for the hospital with reduced visits, a decrease in patient satisfaction, and low company morale.

The board also needed a solution for the physicians acquired in the mergers to seamlessly transition into their compensation plan. But imposing new compensation plans often created stress and conflict, which led to departures.

Lastly, the CEO they brought on just three years ago, who played a vital role in the expansion, was now known throughout the industry and was a target for poaching by reputable competitors for far more money.

Frustrated, the board knew it couldn't be seen as being "held hostage" to pay demands, nor could it commit to big adjustments to match the competing hospitals offer in order to keep their CEO.

Strategy Formulation:
The board needed a solution that incentivized retention, showed appreciation, and was mutually beneficial to the top physicians they wanted to keep. The proposal also had to meet the best interests of the non-profit hospital.

Physicians: ICG wanted to help the board design a plan that would be help guide them towards building a repertoire of key people to their organization. This plan would also protect them when adding new leaders via M&A. Putting a process in place that made newly acquired personnel feel they are in the hands of leaders who would take care of them and lead them to Producer or Legend type status as an employee would be vital to the blueprint this compensation plan.

Below is an example for a 40-year-old, non-smoking male.

Note 1: In this group, some were doctors were specialists who were highly compensated, meaning they were earning more than $1M a year and therefore subject to an excise tax (an *additional* 21% tax at the time this book was written). Any solution that could help avoid that would be a priority.

Note 2: This requires statement that this SERP plan, while informally financed by the company with insurance, is a separate binding legal agreement made between the employer and the employee. As illustrated the company maintains control, meaning the employee has no right to policy values, which are at all times subject to any claims of employer creditors.

ABC Hospital

Supplemental Executive Retirement Plan
IRC Section 7872 Guidelines
Executive / Physician

Initial Death Benefit	$2,911,814.00	
10 Pay WL Premium	$105,000.01	
WL SPIA Purchase	$930,000.00	
Total Loan	$1,035,000.01	

2020 WL Dividend: 6.20%
Dividends are not guaranteed. Policy performance will vary over future years and therefore projected Non-Taxable Benefit will also vary.

Long Term AFR: 2.00%

			Hospital Corporate Account							Executive Account	
		(1) Annual Policy Premium	(2) Total Loan Outlay	(3) Corporate Cash Value	(4) Annual Interest 2.00%	(5) Total Accrued Interest	(6) Corp. DB Loan Repayment Col (2) + Col (5)	(7) Key Man Insurance DB (SPIA DB)	(8) Planned Gift from Exec. DB	(9) Total Corp. Death Benefit	(10) Non-Taxable Benefit (Policy Distb.)	(11) Executive Death Benefit
Year	Age											
1 2020	40	$105,000	$1,035,000	$39,484	$20,700	$20,700	$1,055,700	$930,000	$188,182	$2,173,882	$0	$1,693,642
2 2021	41	$105,000	$1,035,000	$107,132	$21,114	$41,814	$1,076,814	$851,495	$189,746	$2,118,055	$0	$1,707,711
3 2022	42	$105,000	$1,035,000	$207,179	$21,536	$63,350	$1,098,350	$745,058	$192,301	$2,035,709	$0	$1,730,706
4 2023	43	$105,000	$1,035,000	$314,112	$21,967	$85,317	$1,120,317	$638,621	$195,812	$1,954,751	$0	$1,762,308
5 2024	44	$105,000	$1,035,000	$428,309	$22,406	$107,724	$1,142,724	$532,185	$200,257	$1,875,165	$0	$1,802,312
6 2025	45	$105,000	$1,035,000	$547,915	$22,854	$130,578	$1,165,578	$425,748	$204,779	$1,796,104	$0	$1,843,009
7 2026	46	$105,000	$1,035,000	$673,194	$23,312	$153,890	$1,188,890	$319,311	$209,370	$1,717,571	$0	$1,884,331
8 2027	47	$105,000	$1,035,000	$804,542	$23,778	$177,667	$1,212,667	$212,874	$214,052	$1,639,593	$0	$1,926,465
9 2028	48	$105,000	$1,035,000	$942,153	$24,253	$201,921	$1,236,921	$106,437	$218,801	$1,562,158	$0	$1,969,206
10 2029	49	$105,000	$1,035,000	$1,086,382	$24,738	$226,659	$1,261,659	$0	$223,626	$1,485,285	$0	$2,012,630
11 2030	50	$0	$1,035,000	$1,146,802	$25,233	$251,892	$1,286,892	$0	$228,614	$1,515,507	$0	$2,057,529
12 2031	51	$0	$1,035,000	$1,210,289	$25,738	$277,630	$1,312,630	$0	$233,645	$1,546,275	$0	$2,102,801
13 2032	52	$0	$1,035,000	$1,277,027	$26,253	$303,883	$1,338,883	$0	$238,738	$1,577,621	$0	$2,148,641
14 2033	53	$0	$1,035,000	$1,347,157	$26,778	$330,661	$1,365,661	$0	$243,890	$1,609,550	$0	$2,195,009
15 2034	54	$0	$1,035,000	$1,392,974	$27,313	$357,974	$1,392,974	$0	$249,136	$1,642,110	$0	$2,242,228
16 2035	55	$0	$1,035,000	$1,420,833	$27,859	$385,833	$1,420,833	$0	$254,469	$1,675,302	$0	$2,290,220
17 2036	56	$0	$1,035,000	$1,449,250	$28,417	$414,250	$1,449,250	$0	$259,871	$1,709,121	$0	$2,338,843
18 2037	57	$0	$1,035,000	$1,478,235	$28,985	$443,235	$1,478,235	$0	$265,326	$1,743,561	$0	$2,387,937
19 2038	58	$0	$1,035,000	$1,507,800	$29,565	$472,800	$1,507,800	$0	$270,831	$1,778,631	$0	$2,437,479
20 2039	59	$0	$1,035,000	$1,537,956	$30,156	$502,956	$1,537,956	$0	$276,437	$1,814,393	$0	$2,487,934

Continue on Next Page…

Supplemental Executive Retirement Plan
IRC Section 7872 Guidelines
Executive / Physician

Initial Death Benefit	$2,911,814.00	
10 Pay WL Premium	$105,000.01	
WL SPIA Purchase	$930,000.00	
Total Loan	$1,035,000.01	

2020 WL Dividend: 6.20%

Dividends are not guaranteed. Policy performance will vary over future years and therefore projected Non-Taxable Benefit will also vary.

Long Term AFR: 2.00%

						Hospital Corporate Account					Executive Account	
Year	Age	(1) Annual Policy Premium	(2) Total Loan Outlay	(3) Corporate Cash Value	(4) Annual Interest 2.00%	(5) Total Accrued Interest	(6) Corp. DB Loan Repayment Col (2) + Col (5)	(7) Key Man Insurance (SPIA DB)	(8) Planned Gift from Exec. DB	(9) Total Corp. Death Benefit	(10) Non-Taxable Benefit (Policy Disb.)	(11) Executive Death Benefit
21	2040	60	$0	$1,035,000	$1,568,715	$30,759	$533,715	$1,568,715	$0	$282,330	$1,851,045	$0	$2,540,970
22	2041	61	$0	$1,035,000	$1,600,089	$31,374	$565,089	$1,600,089	$0	$288,434	$1,888,523	$0	$2,595,904
23	2042	62	$0	$1,035,000	$1,632,091	$32,002	$597,091	$1,632,091	$0	$294,768	$1,926,858	$0	$2,652,908
24	2043	63	$0	$1,035,000	$1,664,733	$32,642	$629,733	$1,664,733	$0	$301,319	$1,966,052	$0	$2,711,873
25	2044	64	$0	$1,035,000	$1,698,027	$33,295	$663,027	$1,698,027	$0	$308,055	$2,006,082	$0	$2,772,495
26	2045	65	$0	$1,035,000	$1,731,988	$33,961	$696,988	$1,731,988	$0	$299,721	$2,031,709	$75,000	$2,697,490
27	2046	66	$0	$1,035,000	$1,766,628	$34,640	$731,628	$1,766,628	$0	$291,745	$2,058,372	$75,000	$2,625,703
28	2047	67	$0	$1,035,000	$1,801,960	$35,333	$766,960	$1,801,960	$0	$284,090	$2,086,051	$75,000	$2,556,814
29	2048	68	$0	$1,035,000	$1,837,999	$36,039	$802,999	$1,837,999	$0	$276,750	$2,114,749	$75,000	$2,490,747
30	2049	69	$0	$1,035,000	$1,874,759	$36,760	$839,759	$1,874,759	$0	$269,710	$2,144,470	$75,000	$2,427,393
31	2050	70	$0	$1,035,000	$1,912,254	$37,495	$877,254	$1,912,254	$0	$262,976	$2,175,230	$75,000	$2,366,780
32	2051	71	$0	$1,035,000	$1,950,500	$38,245	$915,500	$1,950,500	$0	$256,525	$2,207,024	$75,000	$2,308,721
33	2052	72	$0	$1,035,000	$1,989,510	$39,010	$954,510	$1,989,510	$0	$250,361	$2,239,871	$75,000	$2,253,253
34	2053	73	$0	$1,035,000	$2,029,300	$39,790	$994,300	$2,029,300	$0	$244,474	$2,273,774	$75,000	$2,200,267
35	2054	74	$0	$1,035,000	$2,069,886	$40,586	$1,034,886	$2,069,886	$0	$238,864	$2,308,750	$75,000	$2,149,779
36	2055	75	$0	$1,035,000	$2,111,283	$41,398	$1,076,283	$2,111,283	$0	$233,493	$2,344,776	$75,000	$2,101,433
37	2056	76	$0	$1,035,000	$2,153,509	$42,226	$1,118,509	$2,153,509	$0	$228,347	$2,381,856	$75,000	$2,055,125
38	2057	77	$0	$1,035,000	$2,196,579	$43,070	$1,161,579	$2,196,579	$0	$223,394	$2,419,974	$75,000	$2,010,549
39	2058	78	$0	$1,035,000	$2,240,511	$43,932	$1,205,511	$2,240,511	$0	$218,602	$2,459,113	$75,000	$1,967,422
40	2059	79	$0	$1,035,000	$2,285,321	$44,810	$1,250,321	$2,285,321	$0	$216,816	$2,502,137	$75,000	$1,951,341

This life insurance illustration is not valid unless accompanied or preceded by a Basic Illustration. Refer to the Basic Illustration for guaranteed elements and other important information.

For Full Illustration and downloadable PDF:
www.intuitivecompensation.com/casestudy

<u>CEO</u>: As for their top employee, the CEO, the board knew she was invaluable to their organization and needed ideas for keeping her retained. With our experience in key employee retention, we were able to propose a few plans that would create win/win situations for all parties where one did not seem to exist.

Most of the board members had heard of some of the concepts of the 6th Pillar, but did not have the right support to see them through the details. ICG explained that unlike the other Pillars of compensation, not all forms of compensation are an *expense* to the business or organization. Pay, bonus, benefits, commission and distributions are all an expense. But, with the 6th Pillar, some structures can remain an asset on the books and not an expense is generated to the organization.

Therefore, if a key physician or CEO leaves, then the organization keeps the asset. It can dissolve the "bucket" back into the company, or better yet, use it to recruit a new physician or CEO... who can step right into the "bucket" already in place.

We Provided:
In the end we provided a Split Dollar Loan Regime Plan, where instead of paying them, we loaned the money for the plan to the physician and CEO. With a loan regime, every penny the organization puts into the plan comes back to the hospital with interest.

See sample below and for full supporting documents, please visit:

For downloadable PDF:

www.intuitivecompensation.com/casestudy

ABC Hospital

Supplemental Executive Retirement Plan
IRC Section 7872 Guidelines

Healthcare Executive

2020 WL Dividend: 6.20%
Dividends are not guaranteed. Policy performance will vary over future years and therefore projected Non-Taxable Benefit will also vary.

Initial Death Benefit	$14,611,873.00
10 Pay WL Premium	$800,000.05
WL SPIA Purchase	$7,080,000.00
Total Loan	$7,880,000.05

Long Term AFR: 2.00%

		(1) Annual Policy Premium	(2) Total Loan Outlay	(3) Corporate Cash Value	(4) Annual Interest 2.00%	(5) Total Accrued Interest	(6) Corp. DB Loan Repayment Col (2) + Col (5)	(7) Key Man Insurance (SPIA DB)	(8) Planned Gift from Exec. DB	(9) Total Corp. Death Benefit	(10) Non-Taxable Benefit (Policy Disb.)	(11) Executive Death Benefit
Year	Age										Executive Account	
1	2020	55	$800,000	$7,880,000	$295,306	$157,600	$157,600	$8,037,600	$7,080,000	$668,316	$15,785,916	$0	$6,014,846
2	2021	56	$800,000	$7,880,000	$801,640	$160,752	$318,352	$8,198,352	$6,487,583	$667,414	$15,353,349	$0	$6,006,729
3	2022	57	$800,000	$7,880,000	$1,553,559	$163,967	$482,319	$8,362,319	$5,676,635	$671,180	$14,710,134	$0	$6,040,616
4	2023	58	$800,000	$7,880,000	$2,355,284	$167,246	$649,565	$8,529,565	$4,865,687	$679,809	$14,075,062	$0	$6,118,284
5	2024	59	$800,000	$7,880,000	$3,209,100	$170,591	$820,157	$8,700,157	$4,054,739	$693,000	$13,447,896	$0	$6,237,004
6	2025	60	$800,000	$7,880,000	$4,107,648	$174,003	$994,160	$8,874,160	$3,243,791	$708,275	$12,826,226	$0	$6,374,476
7	2026	61	$800,000	$7,880,000	$5,054,013	$177,483	$1,171,643	$9,051,643	$2,432,844	$725,657	$12,210,144	$0	$6,530,917
8	2027	62	$800,000	$7,880,000	$6,050,281	$181,033	$1,352,676	$9,232,676	$1,621,896	$745,099	$11,599,671	$0	$6,705,893
9	2028	63	$800,000	$7,880,000	$7,099,366	$184,654	$1,537,329	$9,417,330	$810,948	$766,573	$10,994,851	$0	$6,899,159
10	2029	64	$800,000	$7,880,000	$8,204,510	$188,347	$1,725,676	$9,605,676	$0	$790,027	$10,395,703	$0	$7,110,239
11	2030	65	$0	$7,880,000	$8,653,534	$192,114	$1,917,790	$9,797,790	$0	$812,028	$10,609,818	$0	$7,308,256
12	2031	66	$0	$7,880,000	$9,125,345	$195,956	$2,113,745	$9,993,745	$0	$835,087	$10,828,832	$0	$7,515,782
13	2032	67	$0	$7,880,000	$9,357,190	$199,875	$2,313,620	$10,193,620	$0	$807,750	$11,001,371	$0	$7,269,752
14	2033	68	$0	$7,880,000	$9,598,226	$203,872	$2,517,493	$10,397,493	$0	$781,581	$11,179,073	$250,000	$7,034,225
15	2034	69	$0	$7,880,000	$9,848,616	$207,950	$2,725,443	$10,605,443	$0	$756,476	$11,361,919	$250,000	$6,808,288
16	2035	70	$0	$7,880,000	$10,108,637	$212,109	$2,937,551	$10,817,551	$0	$732,430	$11,549,981	$250,000	$6,591,866
17	2036	71	$0	$7,880,000	$10,378,828	$216,351	$3,153,902	$11,033,902	$0	$709,379	$11,743,281	$250,000	$6,384,410
18	2037	72	$0	$7,880,000	$10,659,113	$220,678	$3,374,580	$11,254,581	$0	$687,224	$11,941,804	$250,000	$6,185,015
19	2038	73	$0	$7,880,000	$10,947,551	$225,092	$3,599,672	$11,479,672	$0	$665,562	$12,145,234	$250,000	$5,990,059
20	2039	74	$0	$7,880,000	$11,242,730	$229,593	$3,829,266	$11,709,266	$0	$644,174	$12,353,439	$250,000	$5,797,562

This life insurance illustration is not valid unless accompanied or preceded by a Basic Illustration. Refer to the Basic Illustration for guaranteed elements and other important information.

ABC Hospital

Supplemental Executive Retirement Plan
IRC Section 7872 Guidelines
Healthcare Executive

Initial Death Benefit $14,611,873.00
10 Pay WL Premium $800,600.05
WL SPIA Purchase $7,080,600.00
Total Loan $7,880,600.05

2020 WL Dividend: 6.20%
Dividends are not guaranteed. Policy performance will vary over future years and therefore projected Non-Taxable Benefit will also vary.

Long Term AFR: 2.00%

| | | | | | Hospital Corporate Account | | | | | | Executive Account | |
| | | (1) Annual Policy Premium | (2) Total Loan Outlay | (3) Corporate Cash Value | (4) Annual Interest 2.00% | (5) Total Accrued Interest | (6) Corp. DB Loan Repayment Col (2) + Col (5) | (7) Key Man Insurance (SPIA DB) | (8) Planned Gift from Exec. DB | (9) Total Corp. Death Benefit | (10) Non-Taxable Benefit (Policy Disb.) | (11) Executive Death Benefit |
Year	Age											
21	2040	75	$0	$7,880,000	$11,549,035	$234,185	$4,063,451	$11,943,451	$0	$623,742	$12,567,193	$250,000	$5,613,679
22	2041	76	$0	$7,880,000	$11,863,858	$238,869	$4,302,320	$12,182,320	$0	$603,809	$12,786,129	$250,000	$5,434,285
23	2042	77	$0	$7,880,000	$12,185,953	$243,646	$4,545,966	$12,425,966	$0	$584,275	$13,010,240	$250,000	$5,258,459
24	2043	78	$0	$7,880,000	$12,517,789	$248,519	$4,794,486	$12,674,486	$0	$565,451	$13,239,937	$250,000	$5,089,060
25	2044	79	$0	$7,880,000	$12,858,188	$253,490	$5,047,975	$12,927,975	$0	$547,215	$13,475,190	$250,000	$4,924,931
26	2045	80	$0	$7,880,000	$13,186,535	$258,560	$5,306,535	$13,186,535	$0	$529,623	$13,716,158	$250,000	$4,766,606
27	2046	81	$0	$7,880,000	$13,450,266	$263,731	$5,570,265	$13,450,266	$0	$512,665	$13,962,930	$250,000	$4,613,983
28	2047	82	$0	$7,880,000	$13,719,271	$269,005	$5,839,271	$13,719,271	$0	$496,605	$14,215,875	$250,000	$4,469,441
29	2048	83	$0	$7,880,000	$13,993,656	$274,385	$6,113,656	$13,993,656	$0	$481,579	$14,475,236	$250,000	$4,334,215
30	2049	84	$0	$7,880,000	$14,273,529	$279,873	$6,393,529	$14,273,529	$0	$467,504	$14,741,033	$250,000	$4,207,534
31	2050	85	$0	$7,880,000	$14,559,000	$285,471	$6,679,000	$14,559,000	$0	$453,564	$15,012,564	$250,000	$4,082,077
32	2051	86	$0	$7,880,000	$14,850,180	$291,180	$6,970,180	$14,850,180	$0	$440,576	$15,290,756	$250,000	$3,965,183
33	2052	87	$0	$7,880,000	$15,147,184	$297,004	$7,267,184	$15,147,184	$0	$460,117	$15,607,301	$0	$4,141,057
34	2053	88	$0	$7,880,000	$15,450,127	$302,944	$7,570,127	$15,450,127	$0	$480,352	$15,930,480	$0	$4,323,171
35	2054	89	$0	$7,880,000	$15,759,130	$309,003	$7,879,130	$15,759,130	$0	$501,242	$16,260,372	$0	$4,511,176
36	2055	90	$0	$7,880,000	$16,074,312	$315,183	$8,194,312	$16,074,312	$0	$522,806	$16,597,119	$0	$4,705,255
37	2056	91	$0	$7,880,000	$16,395,799	$321,486	$8,515,799	$16,395,799	$0	$544,868	$16,940,667	$0	$4,903,814
38	2057	92	$0	$7,880,000	$16,723,715	$327,916	$8,843,715	$16,723,715	$0	$567,641	$17,291,356	$0	$5,108,769
39	2058	93	$0	$7,880,000	$17,058,189	$334,474	$9,178,189	$17,058,189	$0	$590,641	$17,648,830	$0	$5,315,769
40	2059	94	$0	$7,880,000	$17,399,353	$341,164	$9,519,353	$17,399,353	$0	$613,304	$18,012,657	$0	$5,519,738

For downloadable PDF:
www.intuitivecompensation.com/casestudy

For a quick visual refresher on this concept:

LEND

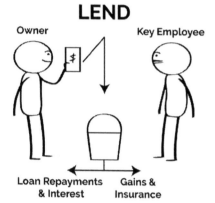

For supporting illustrations, please visit:

www.intuitivecompensation.com/casestudy

Provided By

Design and concept provided by Tom Giltner of Intuitive Compensation Group out of Ohio, and OM Financial a design and servicing partner of Intuitive Compensation Group, out of Boston.

ADDITIONAL RESOURCES

"Even I didn't get it, until I learned
in my own set of circumstances."
- Kevin D. Monaghan

Want Our Help Designing Your Bucket?

Get on Our Schedule & Tell Us Your Story

Call (877) 70-LEARN -

(877) 705-3276

Or via web by going to

www.intuitivecompensation.com

The purpose of this book is not to suggest that the Sixth Pillar is the _best_ option, or that it will solve all your compensation problems. This book and its lessons are meant to serve as a resource to try and make you see compensation from a new perspective. There are lesser known compensation strategies out there that may be able to play a role for you.

When I first heard of the 162 Leverage Executive Bonus I was at a conference, and to be honest, it went way over my head. A confused mind doesn't move forward, and I am no exception. The second time I heard about it was at another conference and I had to sneak in the room because the topic of executive retention was sold out! I still didn't quite get it.

What really fascinated me was why it was sold out and so many people were eager to attend this topic. No other topic at these conferences were selling out and refusing people at the door who wanted to learn. As I chatted with the others in the room, I was shocked to find that so few licensed professionals had ever implemented any of the strategies of the sixth pillar.

As I longed for more information, a mentor of mine sat me down and showed me the concepts of the Sixth Pillar. He explained the variations to me, answering questions along the way, and it allowed me to see how this worked in a set of my own circumstances. I could then picture clearly how this would have impacted my experience in Shanghai. This was the way I needed to hear it. I could relate the structures he was talking about via the emotional pain of my journey in Shanghai.

My reaction was powerful and life changing. After he explained it I looked at him and said, "Why doesn't everyone know about this?" I dropped everything I had going on in my life and started Intuitive Compensation Group, LLC. to help others understand and seek to improve the relationships and clarity with their key people.

It is my belief that the best way to learn about the Sixth Pillar is in a set of your own circumstances. My company would be happy to help you explore what your own numbers could look like for a key person, key people, equity buy-in, buy-out, family business, equity transfer, multi-generational business, Non-Profit, credit union, University, Hospitals paying excise tax on highly compensated doctors, multiple key employees, a leadership team, etc. and walk you through how the Sixth Pillar can work for you, in a set of your own circumstances.

To do so, you can call (877) 70-LEARN, **(877) 705-53276**, or go to www.intuitivecompensation.com to get on our calendar.

Tell us you're story over a 30 minute call, and we'll put to-gether a concept presentation of what your options could look like. From there you'll know if what we do could represent a possible solution for you. We've implemented these from $24/month up to millions. There is no situation too small or too large, we're always happy to help someone who is willing to learn.

If another advisor has given you this book, we are proud that our story may have helped, and we are more than happy to act as a resource for you. We work well with other licensed professionals and are happy to bring our expertise to the table and work alongside them. We are happy to help in any way we can!

Best and thank you,
Kevin D. Monaghan

Disclaimer Page

Disclaimer For Kevin and Intuitive Compensation Group on Tax & Legal Advice

Neither Kevin Monaghan, Intuitive Compensation Group, nor its employees and representatives are authorized to provide tax or legal advice. Individuals are encouraged to seek advise from their own tax or legal professional.

Disclaimer For Kevin and Intuitive Compensation Group.

The views expressed are those of Kevin D. Monaghan. The information provided is not intended and should not be construed as specific tax or legal advice. Kevin Monaghan is an agent of Massachusetts Mutual Life Insurance Company (MassMutual), Springfield, Massachusetts. Intuitive Compensation Group is not a subsidiary or affiliate of MassMutual.

Disclaimer on Accessing the Cash Value inside a Cash Value Life Insurance Policy

Distributions under the policy (including cash dividends and partial/full surrenders) are not subject to taxation up to the amount paid into the policy (cost basis). If the policy is a Modified Endowment Contract, policy loans and/or distributions are taxable to the extent of gain and are subject to a 10% tax penalty. Access to cash values through borrowing or partial surrenders will reduce the policy's cash value and death benefit, increase the chance the policy will lapse, and may result in a tax liability if the policy terminates before the death of the insured. Loan interest is charged when a policy loan is taken. If you take additional policy loans to pay loan interest, your policy's cash/account value will be reduced. At some point, no policy values may be available to pay additional loan interest and out of pocket payments will be required to prevent the policy from lapsing. Failure to pay out of pocket amounts will result in the loss of life insurance coverage and a tax liability in the year of lapse.

REFERENCES

Aguenza, Benjamin Balbuena and Ahmad Puad Mat Som. "Motivational Factors of Employee Retention and Engagement in Organization, Management Journal. Nov-Dec 2012. https://www.managementjournal.info/index.php/IJAME/article/viewFile/233/222

"Albert Frere: Background and Bio." Value Walk Premium. 2018. https://valuewalkpremium.com/albert-frere-resource-page/

Bono. Interview by Larry King. CNN Larry King Weekend. Cable News Network LP, LLC. December 1, 2002.

Buckingham, Marcus, and Coffman, *First, Break All the Rules: What the World's Greatest Managers Do Differently*. New York: Simon and Schuster, 1999.

Chechik, Jeremiah S., dir. *National Lampoon's Christmas Vacation*. 1989; Glendale, CA: Warner Bros, 1997. DVD.

Collins, Jim. *Good to Great: Why Some Companies Make the Leap...And Others Don't.* Harper Business, 2011.

Conversation Staff, "The Real Story of New Coke," The Coca-Cola Company, November 4, 2012, https://www.coca-colacompany.com/history/the-real-story-of-new-coke

Covey, Stephen R. *The Seven Habits of Highly Effective People: Powerful Lessons in Personal Change.* New York: Free Press, 1989.

Deal Stats (26 and 27)

Eldrige, Alison. *Inception*. Encyclopedia Britannica. July 23, 2012. https://www.britannica.com/topic/Inception.

Fincher, David, dir. *The Social Network*. 2010; Andover, MA: Columbia Pictures, 2010. DVD.

Ford, Henry. Due.com. July 1, 2015. https://due.com/blog/henry-ford-customers-pay-the-wages/

Griffin, Jeff, "10 Most Commonly Offered Employee Benefits." JP Griffin Group, February 17, 2017. https://www.griffinbenefits.com/blog/10-commonly-offered-employee-benefits

Guta, Michael. "Number of Businesses Bought and Sold Hit Record Level in 2018." BizBuySell, Jan 27, 2019. https://smallbiztrends.com/2019/01/bizbuysell-annual-2018-insight-report.html

Hedayati, Farnaz. "3 Leadership Qualities of Henry Ford." Center for Work Life, May 7 2014. http://www.centerforworklife.com/leadership-qualities-henry-ford/.

Jio, Kim. "When Does Grab Pay Its Drivers." First Lane. February 7, 2018. https://www.firstlane.com.sg/grab-pay-drivers/

Kohn, Alfie. AZ Quotes. https://www.azquotes.com/quote/1064720

Krasinsky, Susan. "From Healthy Fries to Segways: Why Most Products Fail." The Globe and Mail. September 8, 2014. www.theglobeandmail.com/report-on-business/industry-news/marketing/burger-kings-failed-healthy-fries-campaign-not-unexpected/article20680200/

Maisel, Ivan. "How Jim Harbaugh Made Michigan So Good So Fast." ESPN. October 16, 2015. https://www.espn.com/college-football/story/_/id/13893353/how-michigan-wolverines-got-good-fast-jim-harbaugh

Nassauer, Sarah. "Burger King Tries New French Fries." The Wall Street Journal. September 23, 2013. https://www.wsj.com/articles/burger-king-tries-new-french-fries-1379989427

Pesh, John. "Why Split-Dollar Life Insurance Is Gaining Popularity." August 5, 2019. https://www.cumanagement.com/articles/2019/08/why-split-dollar-life-insurance-gaining-popularity

Pink, Daniel. *Drive: The Surprising Truth About What Motivates Us*. New York: Riverhead Books, 2011.

Poseidon. Bomb Report. 2019. https://bombreport.com/yearly-breakdowns/2006-3/poseidon/

Sapakoff, Gene. "Dabo Swinney gets record $93 dollar contract at Clemson, new Alabama buyout terms." Post and Courier. April 26, 2019. www.postandcourier.com/columnists/dabo-swinney-gets-record-million-contract-at-clemson-new-alabama/article_8bf61320-6833-11e9-bfb2-eba9dc3741fa.html

Schultz, Ellen E. and Theo Francis. "How Life Insurance Morphed Into a Corporate Finance Tool." December 30, 2002. https://online.wsj.com/public/resources/documents/dec_30_one.htm

Shyamalan, M. Night, dir. *The Sixth Sense.* 1999; Philadelphia, PA: Buena Vista Pictures, 2000. DVD.

Stern, Mark Joseph. "A Little Guilt, A Lot of Energy Savings." Slate. March 01, 2013. https://slate.com/technology/2013/03/opower-using-smiley-faces-and-peer-pressure-to-save-the-planet.html

Thompson, Arienne. "Rain Wilson: 'The Office' Kinda Sucked After Steve Carell Left." USA Today. January 22, 3015. https://www.usatoday.com/story/life/entertainthis/2015/01/22/rainn-wilson-the-office-kinda-sucked-after-steve-carell-left/77604532/

Tinubu, Aramide. "What is Steve Carell's Net Worth? Here's What 'The Office' Icon Is Worth Today." ShowBiz Cheat Sheet. November 18, 2018. https://www.cheatsheet.com/entertainment/what-is-steve-carells-net-worth-heres-what-the-office-icon-is-worth-today.html/

"Verifying Motivators." Leading Answers. December 14, 2006. https://leadinganswers.typepad.com/leading_answers/2006/12/verify ing_motiv.html

"When Does Uber Pay Its Drivers." First Lane. January 30, 2018. https://www.firstlane.com.sg/uber-pay-drivers/